Tapestry of Love

A Brother, A Sister, And An Odyssey Through Cancer

Tapestry Of Love

A Brother, A Sister, And An Odyssey Through Cancer

Michael and Heidi Zawelevsky

ISBN-13:
978-1478179528

ISBN-10:
147817952X

For Michael

Your pain washed you free

Old and Wise

As far as my eyes can see
There are shadows approaching me
And to those I left behind
I wanted you to know
You've always shared my deepest thoughts
You follow where I go
And oh when I'm old and wise
Bitter words mean little to me
Autumn winds will blow right through me
And someday in the mist of time
When they asked me if I knew you
I'd smile and say you were a friend of mine
And the sadness would be lifted from my eyes
Oh when I'm old and wise
As far as my eyes can see
There are shadows surrounding me
And to those I leave behind
I want you all to know
You've always shared my darkest hours
I'll miss you when I go
And oh, when I'm old and wise
Heavy words that tossed and blew me
Like autumn winds will blow right through me
And someday in the mist of time
When they ask you if you knew me
Remember that you were a friend of mine
As the final curtain falls before my eyes
Oh when I'm old and wise
As far as my eyes can see

--Eric Woolfson and Alan Parsons

Contents

Preface to the Twentieth Anniversary Edition

Twenty years have passed since Michael passed away at the age of thirty-four in 1992. My future has unfolded in the wake of his loss. Twenty-nine years old myself, at the time of his death, I could not fathom having a future. When I did wonder about it, I felt a transience laden with fear. After all, the past and the present had brought me into the heart of pain and grief, of dying young, so to consider what may be up ahead felt traumatic.

Moving on and healing became my focus, a practice of walking into the future day by day. I walked with friends. I walked with my dogs. I walked on all seven continents, including a charity climb to the summit of Kilimanjaro, the only walk that has left me more winded than trying to keep up with Michael as he sped along on crutches.

I walked and I wrote.

Writing *Tapestry of Love* was its own journey of catharsis and transformation, a journey seen through the kaleidescope of shattered lives made beautiful in spite of and even because of being broken. As our lives have been refracted through time, I have benefitted, even with an eidetic memory, from this task of telling our story, of not only narrating it, but of making a commitment to memory itself because it is still living.

As I sat at my desk to write this preface, the phone rang and it interrupted and distracted me. I looked at the caller i.d. and saw the number was from Beaverton, Oregon. I do not know anyone in Beaverton, Oregon. I let it go to voicemail, but there was no message. And then I got it, remembering how the famed psychic, Sylvia Browne, says that our dearly departed loved ones find ways to contact us, like ringing the phone.

Was it just a missed, unknown call from a telemarketer or a wrong number? Or was it the spirit of my brother, who had been diagnosed twenty years ago to this day, on April 9, 1992, with a recurrence of bone cancer at St. Vincent Hospital which is, geographically, next door to Beaverton, Oregon? It would be the kind of connection if not the kind of prank that he would have loved to pull on his little sister. I can live with the levity, knowing the smile that would steal across his face.

I can also live with the irony of my own personal odyssey as it resonates with the twenty years that transpired in Homer's epic, when Odysseus reveals himself upon his return home, "Twenty years gone, and I am back again." As Michael liked to say, there are no coincidences.

The tragedy of Michael's loss has also had its blessings. In dying young, he gave me an early start on the path of greater healing. I grew up. My sensitivity in life has deepened into a dedication to love in the midst of suffering. This compassion is an affirmation, too, that my brother did not die in vain.

And let me not forget the animals who populate my life and keep the human-animal bond central to my experience. All of my efforts through the years to heal them, in veterinary nursing, have healed my own life. I offer them my gratitude for the loving people who come along with them and renew my sense of community. I offer them my gratitude for their unconditional love, their trust and innocence, for their antics.

The years, then, have tempered how raw Michael's loss felt, but it is always immediate, a presence in my life, for these twenty years have taught me how love and relationships endure and live on. The conversation is undying. I did not run away from the pain of the loss; instead, I walked into it. I walk every day. Perhaps, it is a kind of prayer.

Heidi Zawelevsky
April 9, 2012

Chapter 1 Lifeline

San Francisco International Airport

October 2, 1985

They will go straight down the stairs to Customs. Glass partitions reach up from the stairwell to the ceiling, transparent walls for viewing the stream of arriving passengers. Elderly German couples stand on either side of me, squeezing my small frame until my clothes feel too tight and I am pressed into my own reflection in the glass. My shoulder bag weighs heavily because I cannot shift its bulkiness, keeping such close company with these people and the partition. But my vision is free and moves unobstructed through the crowd of Lufthansa employees and passengers. My eyes wander, search for my brother amid the people who stop momentarily at the top of the stairs. I watch their smiles as they spot their family and friends; watch their laughter, silent within the glass, and I wait.

An attendant pushes an empty wheelchair down the corridor to the plane. I stand, remembering his reason for going to Munich: the knee

1

surgery, a minor repair of the prosthesis that only its German makers could do, a minor repair for nothing more than a loose screw. Cancer free. The wheelchair vanishes, but questions of my brother's mobility overtake my mind and I uncontrollably snap back to an arrival five years ago.

Hysterical family members cry his name over and over, "Mike, oh, Mike!"; cry over the last one off the plane, an exhausted little old man, only twenty-two really but faint, ill, worn. A student abroad, whose campus life became a ten month hospital stay battling cancer, major surgeries, chemotherapy. "Mike, oh, Mike," in a wheelchair, a leg still bandaged, immobile, internally replaced with an artificial knee and platinum spikes for bones. Fainting, falling forward, his weakened body seems to shrink within his suit of light blue pinstripes. I clasp his shoulders and sit him upright.

"I'm o'kay, I'm o'kay." He wakes with his voice and adjusts his wig.

The wig, that blatant feature of his gaunt self, reveals a few stray, original hairs that are now colorless but defiant in their bout with chemotherapy. Straggling signs of the body's outrage at its poisoned life, the strands waver like trees caught in a fire, a blaze that strips away their stature. Vestiges, charred and thin and apparently useless, mark that life has been and still holds on. Life holds on by the roots, surviving but disabled, until the smoke clears and the heat cools and seed forms know it is safe, again, to grow.

I stop my reverie, focus now on the man with crutches; thick black waves of hair, a full mustache and goatee center my attention. Happily

2

waving a crutch, he salutes me with pleased recognition and I know, by his deft signal, that the crutches are only stabilizing his travel weary leg. A short walk and he will not want the crutches or need them. His own stair top pause, like that of the other travelers, gives way to the pull of Customs. Strong and lithe, he moves on, swinging himself rapidly downstairs.

Tall chrome doors slide open, a rush of sound pours from the Customs area and people, whom I recognize from the earlier procession, emerge and then disperse with those whom they have come to see. Soon, hearing my American monotone blend with German accents, my brother and I embrace with a mutual greeting that cannot help its level of understatement, "Good to see you."

"You look great, Michael."

"So do you, little sister. I'm just tired and my hair is too long."

"Minor adjustments."

"Really! I brought you a present from Augsburg's 2000th birthday."

"I brought you a present from my garden's first summer." Jalapenos, which he likes to eat raw.

"Well, I brought you *this*." He waves an invisible gift.

"Well, I brought you *that*."

We exchange a dozen more fictitious gifts of "this and that" as the luggage cart plows our way to the next building, to his connecting flight home to Portland.

3

"I'm world famous, did you hear? I'm the only one in the world, with this knee prosthesis, who fences." We check his luggage and abandon the cart, walking on.

"I haven't exactly read any reviews of your fame, but your letters told of the doctors' reaction to your progress."

"They will be presenting my case to world medical conferences." He rolls his eyes over the doctors' incredulity and excitement. "Look, I told them, I fenced before I had cancer and I'm just going on with my life. Fencing makes me happy, not a celebrity."

"The doctors are probably just a little overwhelmed right now. The odds were so against you..."

He shrugs, anticipating my point. "That's true, I had a tumor with a ninety-eight percent mortality rate."

"And now you're an athlete with an artificial knee; it's o'kay to show people that you have endured and strengthened beyond belief, even if the doctors are showing you off for a while. Did they make a video of you in action?"

"I have to make the video. I have fifty-five fencing students this semester, so there will be plenty of opportunity." He walks without a limp, confident. My attention flags from his movements as I simply listen to him. "Plenty of opportunity."

I gasp, catching sight of him keel over, "MICHAEL..." Reaching to steady him, my attempt fails completely since I also carry his heavy book bag on top of my own. But he has already twirled around a few steps beyond, agile and smiling.

4

"See, the knee works just fine."

"Oh, such a fencer, you were lunging."

"Of course, you think I would fall over?"

"No, of course not, I thought I would."

"On guard!" And he pokes me in the ribs.

We sit together, announced flight arrivals and departures blare often over our conversation; with each departure he angles his head a little more to the loudspeaker, listening for his flight call. Our visit is short but valued and we exchange gifts now.

"I told people you eat these peppers raw."

"I do!" He accepts them proudly.

I hold my commemorative plate of Augsburg's 2,000 years while he asks rhetorically but with reverence, "So, you heard the good news?"

"It's better than good."

"The ordeal is finally over. The cancer has been in remission for five years, it's *gone*." His eyes grin, golden reflectors in the afternoon light.

From the safest vantage point we have ever known, we can view his health. The view is safer this day than four years ago, when he was convinced he no longer had cancer, because time has proven his conviction. Tears of laughter and triumph glide down our faces. The ordeal is over.

Turning to stories of his latest travels, Michael reveals a new treasure, an immense book on Augsburg, and launches into a passionate, condensed narrative history. I am grateful for the book's pictures: "The

5

who? The what?" Augsburg becomes more readily apparent to my mind as I concentrate on a Toblerone candy. I eat the fresh, triangular chocolate backwards. There goes the "R", the "E", the "L" while Augsburg whizzes through the years.

A commemorative plate sits on my lap while he lives with a five year old knee. The history book put away, we realize the juxtaposition. 2,000 years create a deep sense of place, of history and have magnetized him to strong thoughts of continuation. 2,000 years draw him to his own immediate sense of living on.

Five years ago, he recalls, he suffered liver failure from methotrexate, a chemotherapy drug, and slipped beyond coma into death. He registered no signs of life for upwards of a minute.

"You were out of your body?" I ask, offering to put his experience into words.

"What body?" He answers me flatly and then talks of his recent hospital stay where frightened patients, concerned and wanting comfort, sought his insights.

"What was it like being dead?" Hope of an answer sparked in a man's voice.

"Total non-physical oneness, as an individual entity, with the universe. It was so beautiful." Even recounting the story, he lingers on the word *beautiful*, as if the telling moves him again, not only in memory but in actual experience, to this place of connectedness.

The patient, anxiously seeking eternity, leaned forward, "Does the feeling go on forever?"

"I don't know. I wasn't dead forever." Michael is his most factual self.

Both of our heads angle automatically toward the loudspeaker that calls his flight. Just as automatically, we hug and say again, "*Good* to see you."

Michael holds a palm toward me. The lifeline, long and deep, has changed in the last few years from a short, weak imprint. He waves good-bye and springs away on his crutches, using them for speed not stability. I turn to go, my heart on an upbeat, with his life size paradox repeating in my ears, "I wasn't dead forever." Our good-bye is open ended, reveling in the words, "see you soon." We hold to the lifeline.

Chapter 2 Hanging on by a Thread

In 1992, after twelve years of holding to the lifeline, bone cancer again staked its claim on Michael's life. In writing, in anything, I can never reverse what happened. Yet, writing itself is a kind of hope, that much can be gained in narrating what Michael continued to learn from his experiences both unique to his illness and universal to the human condition and from what I, in relation to Michael, have continued to learn.

Cancer was a cruel taskmaster and it taught me about life and death with a vengeance. It ripped me apart as my brother coped with its ravages. I watched and waited and loved. Together, we fought the good fight, the only fight, and walked a path of dignified living and dying.

Whatever the outcome of Michael's recurrence was to be, whether he was restored to health or the disease took his body, we remained raw, exposed to our pain and, therefore to our compassion and no one, nothing, not a disease, not a failing medical system, not any form of insensitivity nor senselessness could break our will to be humane, to love.

We were fortunate and uplifted by the outpouring of care extended by so many, from the doctors, nurses and staff at Klinikum rechts der Isar, University of Munich and St. Vincent Hospital, Portland, Oregon, to our family and friends. We could never be the same not just because of a disease, but because of this gift of love. Ripped apart, we held nothing back and shared a precious closeness with many, melting in it.

Each shift in the pattern of a kaleidoscope is unique and beautiful. Michael, seen through the kaleidoscope of relationship, was many different things to many different people. While this holds true for many people and relationships in general, it was especially pronounced with Michael. The images that people had of him could be so contrasting as to make it hard to imagine that the same Michael was involved and, no doubt, many stories can be told--which is also to say that certain relationships are beyond the scope, the kaleidoscope, of our memoir. This book, this tapestry of love, is one configuration of beautiful forms. It is our story. My brother. His sister. This odyssey.

Michael, adamant that this story of ours is also part of a greater, collective story, voiced his conviction for writing:

Why am I writing this book? What makes me think my story is so special? After all, mine is but one among tens of thousands of like odysseys, odysseys beyond cancer into love and peace. What gives me the right to hold myself up as some example to the world, as if I were some special case among those tens of thousands? Tens of thousands making a heroic go of it, seeking greater meaning and being amid the grief, pain, and fear. Tens of thousands of stories full of nobility and grace, full of love, full of transcendence.

Indeed, why should it be mine that is the voice that is heard? There is really only one reason: namely, I insist the world hear. I insist the world hear because this is not just my story. Because this is not even just the story of me and those who love and support me. I have known so many patients and there is little in my writings that does not apply to so many of those tens of thousands. So many voices, unheard except by those around them.

I want these voices to be heard! It is time a fearful and confused world knows that we are not lepers, that we are not freaks, and even if we die by the hundreds of thousands a year worldwide, we do not surrender. My fellow cancer patients and I are warriors, growing stronger even as our bodies rot, growing compassionate, loving, and peaceful in the face of insensitivity, fear, pain, and grief. And the same holds true for those who walk the path with us. We are millions. And we deserve to be heard, be heard for those who are not.

Michael said to me, "This experience is *more* than a network of people. It's a *tapestry.*" This tapestry is woven with a common thread. As diverse as we all are, this thread is love. For Michael and the unknown lives our story may touch and encourage, I dedicate myself, then and now, to this voice that shall be heard, to this book written, woven into a tapestry of love. Let this story open the door to the life of a man whose courage, dignity, humor, and love transforms all of those who share the journey.

This book is a process of experiencing and understanding, of trying to live and die consciously. It is not a thesis, only an unfolding of the struggle through a cruel disease and the glimmers, even realizations, of what always precedes and exceeds the suffering, and the suffering is immense, often overwhelming and unspeakable.

I do not have any answers, but I articulate this odyssey through cancer as a family member and as a support person. As a friend. By the end of this book, I will have no conclusion, but I will have with Michael a type of never ending story, a human story with an ineffable conclusion. We form two voices in the community of cancer and of humanity, voices which say that love, the love that rips you to shreds, that makes you raw, this love that *hurts* ultimately transforms the cruelty of cancer into love of the true heart; this very heart of compassion from which we are never, ever separate.

Michael wanted only one thing: to be bliss, to be the heart. Ineffable Michael. Ineffable conclusion.

Chapter 3 The Path of Greater Healing

Mt. St. Helens was not the only thing that blew up in 1980. The volcanic landscape of the Cascade Mountains, so integral a part of my Oregon home, reflected my own inner state when I found out that Michael, halfway around the world, had cancer. I looked at Mt. St. Helens, blown apart, and I looked at myself and saw no difference. I realized that little sisters do grow up and that I was doing so just as this mountain had turned into an inferno. Michael's bone cells had erupted and neither one of us would ever be the same again. 1980 had unleashed a cascade of life and death and time.

For the first eight months of Michael's illness, until May, 1981, we were separated by several thousand miles. At his insistence, I stayed in Portland to finish my freshman year in college while he was treated in Munich where he was a student. We kept in touch through the mail and good progress reports came in every few weeks, always encouraging, but never revealing any brutal details. Michael used the physical distance between us for protection, to blunt the agony of sharing his pain, of bringing pain on a loved one. But the autonomy of distance that Michael required was arduous for me to endure. I felt left out (a major sore point for a little sister) of something which I sensed was far more scary than what I was being told, as if I was getting the condensed version of Michael's cancer. It did not help at all that, at the age of seventeen, I did not know how to ask for emotional help and barely had a clue that I could possibly be supported for my feelings. I was a stranger to myself.

I also had put myself in an atmosphere at college that seemed oblivious to my calamity. I was at a small liberal arts college, which Michael had also attended, that focused on one-to-one interaction, but it was academic not emotional. A few friends gave me invaluable support, but no one else reached out to me and many told me, "Have your personal life, but don't let it get in the way of your work." And the few attempts that I did make to express my feelings backfired.

One morning, I saw my advisor in the cafeteria. He also knew Michael. I excitedly told him the news that Michael's tumor had been successfully, completely removed.

"There, you see," he advised me, "it's just been nothing to worry about."

I knew that it definitely was something and perhaps I had a lot less to worry about now, but his dismissive tone was not a form of comfort. Michael's illness was hard enough for me to talk about and I became ever more silent as people failed to respond seriously to the impact that his life threatening illness had on me.

When cancer recurred in 1992, I again did not always find support where I expected it. I felt sure, in 1992, that certain people would respond in my time of greatest need, my greatest pain. But they did not. As I gained distance on my disappointment, however, I felt that perhaps their absence was based in fear, the fear not only of another's pain and mortality, but the pain and mortality reflected in their own lives.

Then again, and one of the greatest lessons, has been the gracious support, the true kindness not only of friends but also of strangers, that has outshined all lack of support, uplifting me, and helping me carry on. Children have been a shining example. I had met Dustin, my coworker Louisa's four year old son, just twice before Michael became ill, but this little boy asked about me everyday after work.

"Was Heidi at work today?"

"Yes, Dustin."

"Was she sad?"

"Yes, Dustin."

"Because her brother's sick?

"Yes, Dustin."

"Is she going to be sad for a long time?"

"I think so."

"I'm sorry."

I still cry when I think of this little boy's unfettered concern and the bear hugs he would give me so that I would know happiness again.

My expectations had little to do with those who cared and those who seemed not to. The primary difference between my experience in college and the recurrence was within myself. If someone or some place was incapable of being supportive, I went elsewhere. I learned to weave this tapestry of love and understand that I am not alone.

But in 1980, Michael had thousands of miles as a buffer zone and I respected his space; my hard schoolwork supposedly took precedence over "the rest" of my life, and I reflexively withdrew into myself, towing the line of what I perceived to be everyone's expectations of me. Finding my way out of myself, taking those first tentative steps on the path of greater healing, only began when I heard a certain comment during a biology lecture on genetic diseases, cancer included, in the Spring of 1981.

With joy, the visiting professor said, "These people are self-destructive. We geneticists just *love* to study these diseases because they are *so devastating*." She paused with an awkward look on her face, the passion for her specialty lost in the ensuing silence.

I had been walking around in silent shock, unable to talk about how threatening Michael's cancer was to me, but I knew on a gut level, where the professor's words had hit me, that Michael did a lot more than fascinate me. I loved him and I was in terrible pain over the tenuous finality of his life. The devastation of knowing that I may lose my childhood counterpart had filled me with despair, but when I heard this statement on biological deviances, I knew that I could no longer stuff my feelings about Michael's illness.

Michael returned to the States shortly after The Lecture. He left his friends in Munich, his support base, because he had fallen in love with a woman on the East Coast whom he had met once. They had become pen pals after meeting on an airplane in 1979 and, during his long hospitalization, she wrote him beautiful, romantic letters, called him on the phone, and together they built dreams of a glorious relationship. He was crazy about her, but after they were together only a few weeks, their relationship disintegrated. She was not quite the princess he had envisioned. To her, he was sexually inadequate and less than a man because of the crippling effects of cancer. Devastated, Michael returned home to Oregon to complete chemotherapy and rehabilitation.

Michael and I, reunited, now faced just how good we both were at being tough guys, knowing in essence that we were no better than the Lion in *The Wizard of Oz* crying, "Courage. Courage." Our masks of strength, of going it alone, crumbled. We had to learn a greater truth about survival because death had knocked on our door and given us an ultimate choice: stop being weak enough to hide our strengths and start being strong enough to expose our weaknesses. We braved sharing our pain and once we did that we shared in a renaissance of healing.

We hit the ground running. Michael became a speed demon on crutches and I raced around town, jogging or bicycling to keep up with him. His determination to regain his health and the full use of his right leg was absolute. Day by day, he logged the miles, only stopping for rounds of chemotherapy that continued through the summer. If something presented itself as an obstacle, he went through it not around it.

"What are you *doing*, Michael?" Our sister, Cheryl, disturbed by a steady banging sound in the house had traced the noise to our big brother. Cheryl spoke with such alarm that I came into the hall with her.

"I'm going up the stairs," he replied and continued laboring with his crutches.

Cheryl and I cheered him on, watching his every move as he climbed not just these stairs but *stairs* for the first time since his surgery several months ago.

The most gruesome aspect of Michael's cancer experience, chemotherapy, was also no longer lost on me. In the early 1980s, before the advent of more effective anti-emetic drugs, Michael endured violent nausea. I learned one of his favorite remedies from Munich, chamomile tea, and kept busy during these seemingly endless bouts of nausea by making pots of tea. Drinking the chamomile helped soothe him, the liquid kept him hydrated and also kept something in his stomach. It also served my need to be involved.

My isolation from Michael's illness that had plagued me for eight months dissolved in my close proximity to all things physical. A gallon of tea, violent nausea, a bald head, crutches. Michael. Sharing the pain. While it is true that Michael waited long enough to develop his own survival skills and to know that he would most likely live, he and I never went back to that initial pattern of separation. Michael nearly died learning this, but it is a lesson we both lived and learned.

At the end of the summer, Michael, with an expression of pure joy, told me that he had had a vision. While he sat in bed early that morning, the room became enshrouded in fog. Through the fog, he began to make out the shape of a large gate in the distance. The gate became clearer and closer until he was right before it. Then the gate swung open and Michael, the entire room, became radiant with a golden light. In the core of his being, Michael knew that he was healed of cancer.

We had a future again.

Chapter 4 The Wound of Love

A cascade of life and death and time. Michael had been in remission for so many years that by 1992 I thought of the word *cancer* only in association with the word *free*. Twelve years had gone by and the suffering of our youth was history. Our adult lives were flowering in the early 1990s, cancer free. Yet the Spring of 1992 brought with it the chill of the past. Throughout March, the present seemed to coincide with events of twelve years ago. I felt like I was repeating myself, but none of it made sense.

I again wanted to be a veterinarian just like twelve years ago when I was a college freshman, but then, in 1980, my ineptitude in chemistry ran head on into my aptitude for literature, landing me in the English department. I had transferred out of the college in Portland, in 1983, and moved to the San Francisco Bay Area, finishing my undergraduate degree in English Literature. I wanted to find a balance with my writing life and my love of working with animals. In time, that would mean a career in veterinary nursing, but in the early 1990s, I was trying to take the science pre-requisites for vet school itself.

As I stood in the line at the bookstore with a genetics textbook, I noticed that it was written by the professor who had been on sabbatical at the school in Portland when I heard those famous words in the biology lecture, "These people are self-destructive...". Thank God that's over, I thought.

In late March, at the pet hospital where I worked, I x-rayed a limping Golden Retriever. I put the radiograph on the light board and saw that she had the extreme misfortune of having a bone tumor.

My co-worker told me with distress, "These tumors are very aggressive. Very lethal."

"I know, my brother had osteosarcoma twelve years ago. He was very lucky. He's doing great."

A few other vets had come into the room by then and were captivated as I told them how Michael had survived bone cancer, how he was literally a walking miracle with his state of the art knee prosthesis.

Later in the day, I walked through the parking lot and saw the Golden Retriever limping along with her family. That poor dog with bone cancer haunted me. 1980 did not feel like my distant past anymore, but I still did not make a direct connection with Michael and the hip pain he had just told me he was having.

His left hip, he had said, was just bruised, having compensated for his right leg with the new knee prosthesis since last summer. What he did not tell me was that his hip had popped out one night in mid-March when he got up to pee, that he had fallen on the bathroom floor, knocked himself out, and woken up in a pool of urine. But whatever he did or did not tell me was eclipsed by the tiredness in his voice. It lingered in my mind, nebulously harassing me.

Still, all of these reminders of life twelve years ago were just that. Reminders. I had not a conscious clue that they were warnings until the last Saturday of the month when everything added up and finally screamed: RECURRENCE!

"Heidi," my housemate, Beth, said, "Michael called while you were at work."

"He did?"

"He said he won't be home tonight, so call back tomorrow."

"O'kay."

"He said, he's having a CAT scan to check for tumors on Tuesday."

Check for tumors. I sat stunned. He had had all of the diagnostic tests for cancer last summer. He was fine.

"*Why are they checking for tumors?*"

"He didn't say. His voice was upbeat." Beth looked miserable as she realized that I was devastated by what seemed to be yet another message from Michael about his continuing medical adventures.

"His voice was *upbeat?* Upbeat and they're checking for tumors!" Don't kill the messenger, I had to remind myself.

"I'm sorry," Beth said.

Dazed, I got up from my chair. Didn't Michael handle all of that nicely? I could not even get ahold of him for another day to find out *what the hell is going on.* I had to get out of the room, get away, if only to the hall. Why had he called? Why would he say that and in an upbeat

21

tone? He had just told me two days ago that he was accepted as a patient by Sisters of Providence, a non-profit Catholic organization with medical centers in the Western United States. As a routine exam for new clients with a history of cancer, he was scheduled to see an oncologist at St. Vincent Hospital in the coming week. I already knew all that.

Something else was going on, something was wrong, more so than structural orthopedic problems. Tumors? I feared that cancer was no longer history and I cried all night.

Sunday morning at work, one of the veterinarians tried to reassure me that bone cancer very rarely comes back in a part of the body other than the original site. Since the original site was replaced with a prosthesis, I should not worry. But Michael was always the long shot and I insisted that he would not call if something was not dangerously wrong.

Work passed like slow torture and I left early to call my brother.

"Hi, Michael. It's Heidi. What is going on?"

"I don't know. Things are getting rough."

"I thought everything was routine."

"That was before the latest report from Germany. I had x-rays taken of my legs and hips and sent the films to my German doctors just before Sisters of Providence accepted me."

"Right, and you said it looked like massive bruising to your hip."

"The radiologist in Munich said that my left hip has extensive lesions and based on my prior history of osteosarcoma, I'd better get myself to an oncologist."

"So the radiologist doesn't think it's bruising?"

"He's not sure. Because of my previous history it could be osteogenic osteosarcoma."

"Osteogenic?" I knew that meant something really bad.

"Yes."

"How extensive a lesion?"

"Extensive."

"One centimeter? Three centimeters?"

"Extensive." Michael's voice was tight.

"What do you feel it is? Do you have any hits on it?"

"No, I honestly don't. Because it really doesn't matter."

"*Really?*" He amazed me with such kindness in his positive tone.

"I don't want a diagnosis of cancer, but whatever is going on I will deal with it. If I have to start chemotherapy tomorrow then I'll pack my bags and go to the hospital. If it's massive bruising then I'll rest until it heals."

"You sound really clear, Michael, but I've been really upset because you just left a message in an upbeat voice with Beth about checking for tumors."

"I'm sorry, I upset you. I didn't mean to at all. Please, apologize to Beth, too, o'kay?"

"O'kay. It's such a relief to hear that you really do feel so positive."

"Well, I keep thinking of a Star Trek episode where a planet is about to be destroyed. A crewmember says to the Captain, 'Captain, is everyone on that planet going to die?' And the Captain, says, 'Everyone is going to die sometime. It's just a matter of when.'"

"I hope that *when* is not now, Michael."

"Heidi, everyone can live with dignity. Everyone can die with dignity. That's all I want. And if this is cancer, I'm going to beat it."

His conviction calmed me down. "I know you can and you *are* dignified. You are so dignified."

"That's all I want. Please, wait for me to call on Thursday. All of the test results will be in Thursday afternoon. Just wait for me to call at six o'clock."

"O'kay, I'll wait."

"I love you."

"I love you, too."

For the next few days, I felt like my heart would explode from the pressure of waiting for the diagnosis. My body surged with electricity and as positive as Michael was, as much clarity as he had, I could not sleep and I could not eat. I was totally wired.

Thursday, April 9, at six o'clock, I stood before the phone. It rang promptly and I froze inside.

"Michael."

"Heidi, it's bad." Our voices were soft.

"It's cancer."

"Yep. And I have it in my hip and in my bladder and in my lungs."

With each part of his body mentioned, I felt more and more sick to my stomach. The dread of the disease.

24

"How are you?" I asked, each word measured with care.

"I'm tired of this," he started to cry. *"I'm tired of this!"*

"I know you are. Oh, Michael, I'm *so sorry*." We were both bawling.

"I'm tired of this!"

Michael choked on his words, "The hardest thing about this is how much *pain* it brings to those I love." He was calling and writing to everyone that night.

"It's a wound of love, Michael. We all love you so much and we're going to be right here with you through all of this."

"O'kay," he sobbed.

"It's a wound of love. I love you. Please, don't worry about causing me pain."

"I love you, too. O'kay."

"We won't be thousands of miles apart this time and the moment you need me just let me know and I'll fly or drive to be with you."

He just cried.

"I'll come right now if you want me to."

"I want you to come soon, but this is so disruptive anyway. I don't want you to have to drop everything right now."

"I'll come really soon."

"Good."

Michael told me that the extensive pelvic lesion seen on x-ray was a fifteen by eight centimeter tumor. The damn thing was the size of a softball. The only good news came a few days after the initial diagnosis when we found out that his bladder was cancer free. It had only appeared diseased because the pelvic mass was pushing into it. But that dark night of diagnosis we knew enough: we were up against the wall. Metastatic bone cancer. Damn it.

"Michael, I think it's a really sick joke that you have a softball sized tumor when cancer plays hardball."

"Yeah," he laughed, "I'm a semi-lethal pain in the ass."

"No, shit."

"But I'm gonna play hardball right back."

"I believe in you."

"I love you, dearly."

"Michael, I really think you should write your story. I know you've been reluctant in the past because you wanted to leave cancer behind, but it's back and your story could help someone else. Your doctor even said that you should write a book."

"I've decided to write it. I want you to write it with me. This is *our* story, Heidi. I can't write it without you."

I burst into tears all over again. "You know that I have always felt so strongly, before I even knew the alphabet, that I would write my first book by the time I'm thirty."

"I know."

"I just didn't want it to come at such a price! I don't want to lose you, Michael!" I was crying so hard I could barely speak.

"You won't lose me. You will never lose me."

"You really mean it."

"Of course, I do. You will never lose me."

Just like twelve years ago, Michael's lifeline was now a short, weak imprint. Broken. But unlike twelve years ago, we promised not to stray from each other, from this path of greater healing. As filled with pain as the night of diagnosis was, it was a night filled too with the promise of love.

"Michael, before you go is there anything else I can do for you right now, tonight?"

"Yes. Start writing."

I went and got a pen.

Chapter 5 Pre-Existing Conditions

Michael, a modern day renaissance man, grew up in the United States like a fish out of water. If he had spent his childhood and youth in a cosmopolitan city like New York or San Francisco, rather than the culturally quiet surroundings of Oregon in the 1960s and '70s, he could have better availed himself of his great loves of classical music and art, foreign languages, European baroque history. I grew up expecting him to move to another country and that day came in 1978, his junior year of college. He had qualified for a year abroad at the University of Munich. Michael boarded the plane, a beret smartly angled on his head. He was bound for Europe, least of all for academics, most of all for the competition of the classical style of fencing and the thriving world of classical music.

"Even the church doors squeak Latin," he said, thrilled with the living past.

He gallivanted across the land to the concert halls and museums of Munich, Salzburg, and Florence, immersing himself for two years in the goldmine of European culture. The last thing that this renaissance man thought he would immerse himself in was the high technology of modern medicine.

In the Fall of 1980, Michael helped his best friend, Hans-Joachim, make a recording of Muffat's music, played on the historic organ of Fuerstenfeld church. Michael's future as part of the classical music scene in Germany seemed full of promise. And then his right knee started to hurt. Too many hours, he thought, of kneeling on a cold stone church floor. Not enough fencing. But his knee continued to hurt, the pain intensifying. It got so bad that he could barely walk. Churches, concert halls, and fencing matches were about to be replaced with a classical disease--cancer--and the medical warfare of surgeries, chemotherapy, and learning to walk again. That Michael was in Munich on a student visa was a life and limb saving stroke of luck when he was diagnosed with a bone tumor just above his knee. Had he been treated in the States, his leg would have been amputated.

He got off to a contentious start with the chief orthopedic doctor, Dr. Hipp, because Michael wanted to know everything about his own case, his own life. Feeling that he was not being told just how severe his form of cancer was, he waited until the middle of the night, then challenged German medical authority. He dragged himself out of bed, his right leg swathed in bandages, swung himself on crutches to the nurses station, and broke the lock on the file cabinet. Dr. Hipp found Michael the next day sitting in bed with his medical records and a medical dictionary. The doctor blew up, Michael blew up back at him, and they went on without secrets, forming a close, helping relationship that lasted the rest of Michael's life.

Michael healed in the early 1980s and with the exception of that loose screw in 1985 the years went by without a hitch. Then hell started breaking loose again when his knee prosthesis broke in May 1991. With his painful leg in a brace, he had to give up his job as a fencing coach while he searched for medical help. Legal and monetary obstacles were the biggest impediments to a prosthesis replacement in the U.S. Michael's insurance would not cover a pre-existing condition, let alone a prosthesis still experimental in the U.S.; the government would not give him assistance; he could not afford the tens of thousands of dollars need to pay for the prosthesis and its replacement here; the risk of malpractice to his American orthopedic doctor was too high. Again, he had a choice between an amputation in the States or a prosthesis replacement at Klinikum rechts der Isar in Munich. The hospital was willing to work out a payment plan and Michael scraped together $2,500. He flew to Munich in July. The new knee went in on August 1. It would take up to a year to regain complete use of his knee.

Michael checked out of the hospital, confused when a nurse handed him his deposit check.

"Dr. Hipp says it's on the house."

Michael returned to Portland and took a steady downhill ride to bankruptcy court. Surviving on unemployment, sending out resumes to German companies because he felt too medically at risk to live in

America anymore, he again tried to receive government assisted healthcare for his disability.

"Do you have cancer?" A social services agent asked him.

"No. I have an ongoing orthopedic disability as a result of having had cancer."

"If you had cancer now, you might have a better chance of receiving assistance."

*If you had cancer now...*Those words came to haunt him, a full-fledged member of the American medical poor. But again, he was lucky, hearing about Sisters of Providence in March of 1992. Sisters of Providence wanted their patients to have exhausted all other financial possibilities before they would provide healthcare. I worried that Michael had exhausted his very life in the process of exhausting all other financial possibilities.

Michael's medical biography is inseparable from the crisis in American healthcare. He more than once got lucky, in Germany in 1980, a country with a single payer medical system and world leading orthopedics, lucky always to be able to turn to Klinikum rechts der Isar, and lucky in 1992 to find the non-profit, charitable Sisters of Providence. His luck, however, did not take away the fear, pain, and humiliation of having to scrounge in this country for healthcare and, more than once, come up empty handed.

Even with insurance, he was denied coverage for his "pre-existing, experimental" orthopedic condition when something went wrong. His difficulties were agonizing, the stress counterproductive to healing, and unnecessary. The worst aspect of his experience is that it reflects what millions of American must suffer. Michael's relationship with Klinikum rechts der Isar afforded him the luxury of healthcare if all else failed in the United States. American medicine has become so unaffordable and inaccessible that millions of Americans may as well live in a third world country.

Sisters of Providence is a beautiful example that healthcare can be humanely given to all in need.

"I feel like I should become an honorary Catholic," Michael said, referring to Sisters of Providence and the Knights of Malta which gave him a place to recuperate in Germany in 1991.

Michael's healthcare came down to desperate luck. Humane care is not ordinarily given freely in the United States, but threatened to be taken away if you cannot afford the exorbitant costs of insurance or the exorbitant costs of medical care. Michael embraced the chance to heal his relationship with the American medical community and that embrace was a searing reminder of our conversation the night of the diagnosis.

"I will not be made to beg for my right to medical care again," Michael was crying in anger. "I have always wanted to heal my relationship with the American medical community and I will not be *humiliated* by these people!" he cried.

"No one will humiliate you now. It sounds really good with the St. Vincent's people and you've really connected with your doctor. He's treating you for free because he wants to."

"Yeah," his voice cracked.

"If it ever does happen where things aren't right here, we'll take you back to Munich."

"That's what I'll want."

"That's what we'll do."

Michael deeply respected his oncologist, Dr. Mastanduno, for taking him on for free, treating him because he was a human being. He characterized his oncologist and his oncology resident, Dr. Frank, as two people who took the Hippocratic Oath and lived by it. Doctors like these, hospitals like St. Vincent, are a calm in the storm of American healthcare.

The power of insurance companies to drop someone or refuse to pay for certain needs makes me wonder why we use the word *insurance* at all. The breakdown of medical costs that need to be covered are themselves a blur. Michael needed a hospital room, medication, consultations (one of which billed him one hundred dollars for a physical therapist at St. Vincent to watch him flex his knee for less than five minutes), chemotherapy, radiology, oncologists, urologists...the list was exhaustive. The hospital picked up all expenses until Medicaid came through in mid-July, but--oops--Medicaid forgot to pay for in-hospital care, covering only doctor visits and prescriptions. St. Vincent continued to pick up the fifteen thousand dollar tab for Michael's hospitalizations until Medicaid was straightened out through the hard efforts of a St. Vincent social worker.

But he was still left in the lurch at home. By July, state disability awarded him two hundred and sixty odd dollars a month. He received food stamps, too. The money from the state helped a little, but it was not nearly enough, certainly not for a critically ill person. We struggled to provide Michael with the most basic health needs at home, another blur of costs for massage therapy, cotton bedding, an air conditioner, and toiletries.

How can anyone find the peace of mind and dignity to focus on healing when burdened with the anxiety of how to cover life saving health needs? How does a leukemia patient tell her child that she missed out on her best chance of survival because she does not have the six figures to pay for a bone marrow transplant? How many bake sales do we have to have in this country to raise money for our sick loved ones before a single payer system, not a cure all but a most sensible and compassionate form of healthcare, goes into effect?

The CBS program, *48 Hours*, broadcast a show on breast cancer in 1991. Michael and I talked about this for a long time because it illustrated how the healthcare system fails people. It does no good for the poor, African-American woman in Harlem who felt a lump in her breast for a year before she sought medical help. She was afraid for her health, but she was just as afraid to lose her job that paid little more than six dollars an hour, not much but all she had, all a lot of us have. Where is she now? This poor, minority woman with metastatic breast cancer. Michael and I thought further of the poor, the elderly, the ethnic minorities, and the most socially stigmatized group, people with AIDS. We thought, too, of ourselves, what it had been like already and what if, God forbid, it could be again.

Michael repeatedly put the cruelty of the current system in strong terms, "Who are these people to hand out death sentences? This is *genocide*."

The caseworkers assigned to Michael from the various government social services agencies were all good, helpful people. They did their best to provide assistance, but they were as disabled by the bureaucracy as Michael was disabled by his body. Social Security, out of its tangled bureaucratic web, did finally award Michael a monthly stipend, enough to live on. The date of the award was the day that he died.

Chapter 6 Round 2

April 13, 1992

This spacious single room's windows grant me a lush view of an expansive woods, and in the distance lies the dark silhouette of Oregon's jagged Coast Range. There is a luxuriant, verdant calm to the view: cool, enticing. But here, too, are the familiar accouterments of an adjustable bed, blood pressure cuff, oxygen and vacuum outlets, and call switch (the original panic button...). The television mounted on the wall leers blackly down at me like some futuristic monitoring device. And, of course, there is the omnipresent, cloying odor of disinfectants. All these serve as potent reminders that this is neither a ski nor ocean resort, but rather a last resort. It is the place of miseries and of desperate hopes that the folks in white will pat you on the back as you are discharged, uttering the word "healed" as you venture back into the "real" world of the healthy.

Health: a world I departed abruptly last May to the metallic "snap" of part of my ten year old knee prosthesis as it irreparably bid its molecular bonds to the rest of the device a destructive farewell. Then came two months of generously being offered an amputation at the hip for the bargain price of $8,000 because my insurance company decided that a pre-existing condition was the perfect excuse to play hide-and-don't-go-seek. ("Oh, and do not forget to send in your $122/month premium, sir!") To make matters worse, the U.S. government did not deem my situation serious enough to merit their assistance, and I just could not bring myself to rob a bank for the $45,000 needed to replace a defunct device.

After all the desperation and fear that I was about to lose my limb, I was invited back to Germany. "We will take care of you, so do not worry about your leg or your finances," they said.

Out with the old, in with the new, and off to the countryside for recuperation. It was almost that simple--until I returned to the U.S. of A, and found myself out of house and home, and job, and healthcare. Last month came the dislocation of my hip and another frantic round of trying to arrange for healthcare until I found the gracious kindness of Sisters of Providence. It was not a moment too soon.

Osteogenic osteosarcoma. A bone-producing bone tumor. Not even my most morbid imaginings could have contemplated having to go through cancer again, especially since getting it a second time is usually a death sentence. During the week and a half between x-ray, CAT scan, and the final diagnosis, I found myself being reasonably certain that my hip popping out caused massive bruising to the pelvis. Yes, there was some denial in that, but there was no denying that I was losing mobility in my left hip and was starting to have shortness of breath. When I saw the CAT scan, I knew. Only the prognosis--and treatment--lay ahead.

I am going to beat it again, even though a little voice keeps taunting me that I am a dead man. Of course, I am a dead man. I have been a dead man for twelve years. But I am also a free man, free of the fear of death. If my body loses this battle, I shall go back into that endless bliss of non-corporeality, non-needfulness, and universal unity I was so fortunate to have briefly experienced over a decade ago. I have this sense of peace and calm that is mostly unshaken by this illness. Yes, there was great sorrow when I learned of the diagnosis and I did my share of crying. I learned the great lesson of a dozen years ago: deny nothing, hide nothing, let it go. You must share yourself, your hopes, your fears, your sorrows, your joys, all of your life, and, in the end, all of your death.

Cancer is not just a journey through misery and, possibly, death, but one of courage and love. Cancer is a challenge to trust: to trust yourself, to trust others. No armor against the experience exists and walls only close you in and others out, leaving you cut off, isolated, and damnably alone. No one goes through this alone. At the very least there is the medical staff. There is also family and friends. In one sense, it is terribly sad to know you cannot shield and protect your loved ones from the suffering. At the same time, endless comfort comes from knowing that others care so deeply for you that your suffering is their pain, too.

The only gratitude appropriate is in not cutting them off, letting them share in your struggles, assisting you in any way they can, and for you to trust and love them, to support each other. Ultimately, each of us is responsible for our own reactions and feelings, but sharing grants needed credence and legitimacy. Strength comes from people helping support each other.

Please, trust me in this. I tried the macho route, the lone hero as epitomized in Norse sagas, the first time. It was a worse poison than chemotherapy and it still has residual ill effects on my life to the present moment.

Chapter 7 2:44 a.m.

April 19, 1992

So much for my first night out of the hospital after my first round of chemotherapy. There is really nothing like a good, disorienting nightmare, you know, the roller coaster ride through la-la hell and places to send mortal souls screaming for cover, to make you decide that lights on and something cogent and deliberate like writing is the closest thing to heaven on Earth. No drippy, oozy cadaverous things. Just two GE 67 watt light bulbs, a pad of paper, a pen, and a will not to go mad.

I am very calm, actually. Twelve years of life on the edge has a way of encouraging that in a person, and the old instincts are returning. How to cope. How to fight. But this is odd and it has been since all this resumed two weeks ago. The "this" to which I am referring is desperation. Twelve years ago, when I was a child dying of cancer, I was desperate to survive, to survive at any cost. Now, I am something more than a child dying of cancer. I am living of cancer (grammar be damned). Cancer as an allegory of my life. Of all that has been twisted, perverted, and rotted in it. There is no accusation or denunciation in this, just a realization--one made in absolute clarity--that to heal myself of cancer is to heal my soul. To make peace, even to live in peace with pain. To forgive. To accept. To transcend. To just be a human being for a change.

There is no desperation in me. If I cannot simply be, then life is a useless struggle fraught with suffering, leading to a dry mouth full of ashes. Perhaps later this will all seem surreal to me, re-reading this, but at this moment, my path is simple, painless, and clear. I shall simply be whatever I am. Now, I have some vague notions from what I have done with my life: translator, teacher, swordsman, musician, computer programmer. But, what does that really mean? Are we just the sum total of our actions and thoughts? Most human beings seem to think so (ever go into a bar: "so whadda you do?"). Sorry. Perhaps I am trivializing life for others by imagining my proximity to death somehow sets me apart, drives *me*, that special indefinable *me* to seek Tao, Buddha, Christ, or the True Nature of the Cosmic Wizzbang. But there is no Tao. No Buddha. No Christ. No Cosmic Wizzbang (with or without true nature). No special me. Just, thank God, a me. And for now, that is all I can comprehend. And it is wonderful. So what that I have cancer. I am, and I am content with that. For the first time in my life, I am content, for I understand now what I have been striving for all these years, knowing that the moment is at hand and that I am here for it.

Healing. To shed old pains. To forgive old sins and sinners. To step out into the light and say, "so it goes." And to be content. Healing is a state of burdenlessness. A way of being whole in spite--or even because--of anything, everything. To simply live. To simply be. To simply do. Simply content.

My hair is getting waxy again and my mouth has a coating of slime. There is bile in my stomach and my tumor hurts. It doesn't matter. I am content. I am me. And that, I do believe, is all I ever wanted.

Only one prayer: may I never forget.

3:44 a.m.

Chapter 8 The Path of Greater Pain

Michael repeated his prayer of remembrance when a particularly miserable day two months into his recurrence triggered the terror of the onset of cancer in 1980...

June 24, 1992

If anyone tells you that battling cancer isn't so bad, that it isn't an ordeal, they are either liars or idiots, excepting those with extremely mild cases not requiring the usual and customary brutal intervention. And if anyone gets the impression that because I have found peace and happiness I am having an easy go of it, you might want to see how I painfully wretch up immense amounts of mucous every day, to collapse in an exhausted heap in bed for hours on end, incapable of even shifting my position. Or the agony of trying to sit or stand up as muscles get dragged over my tumor's boney shell. Or not being able to bend over. Or not to be able to dress myself. Or to find that brushing my teeth leaves me winded and needful of an hour's lying down. I will spare you further details, but suffice it to say that whatever I do, including trying to write this book, it is just damnably difficult.

A recent sample of the bigger picture is no more pleasant. One and a half weeks of massive lung infections thanks to a housemate who left rotting food lying around and has since been evicted for being hazardous to one's health. One week of chemotherapy during which I had respiratory distress serious enough to require that my right lung be drained. The lung collapsed and I got to spend another week in the hospital with a large plastic tube in my chest. Now, I am bedridden at home. There isn't much left of me, physically (I'm now at least 5 % underweight), and long meditations are no substitute for recuperative sleep, which is hard to get when you can only lie on your back and that means lying on a massive bone tumor or lying on a side that has a couple of holes in it from chest tubes. I feel like God stepped on me.

At least, I am not puking my guts out--yet.

What about when your immune system is shot? You wind up relatively isolated because having visitors poses a serious risk of infections, as does going outside. God damn it, you cannot hug someone over the phone, or see his/her smiles, cry on his/her shoulder, or anything else. And when your cancer has invaded your lungs, you cannot even talk very long, either on the phone or in person (this must be divine retribution for my having been a blabber-mouth all these years).

Let's not even begin discussing terror, grief, anger, the feeling that your own body has betrayed you, the sense of helplessness, people losing

44

it emotionally, the pain, the denial, and all that. It is just too depressing, other than to say that everyone goes through it.

Cancer is one hell of an ordeal, and a mercilessly cruel one, and even if you and those who support you find a way to make more of this than the physical ordeal, that is to say, turn cancer into an odyssey, a healing, transcendent experience, it still remains an ordeal.

Going beyond the ordeal of cancer and into the odyssey was a hideously painful and terrifying lesson to learn. Perhaps it was needful of me to be terrified into seeking something else, something better, something higher. After all, I was locked into a cycle of suffering that only begat more suffering and the spiral had finally tightened into a strangle-hold. While that cycle was indeed broken, transcended, the road I have had to travel belongs to the worst Hell imaginable, and the journey began in the blinding darkness of mad terror, ravaging pain, and crushing degradation. It began as follows.

Daymares
Munich
November 3, 1980

The testing for the cause of the terrible pain in my right leg took several days, then the doctors told me to go home, pack my bags, and wait by the phone. The cancerous tumor they found must come out--immediately. All they needed was a bed for me. Just a bed--and so I wait. And wait.

Please, ring...please. I'm scared. Try to breathe. Stay calm. God help me. I don't want this. It isn't happening. Please, ring. Breathe.

I...don't...want...to...die...Just breathe. Pack your bags and wait by the phone...I did that two days ago. Oh, please, ring...please.

Last night, a friend let me cry myself to sleep in her lap. She stayed all night, a guardian angel. She is still awake when I arise, still has that same expression of grief-ridden compassion. How will Uli's pretty face look, I wonder, when I have no hair and am an emaciated husk? Blessed mother of god! Is that how I am going to look? Someone please help me...I'm scared.

Ring, you god-damned bastard, ring!

My housemates are as scared as I am. Why? They are not being eaten by their own bodies. I'm the one. Not them. Please don't let it be them. They are my friends. I need them.

Please, ring.

The brrrt-brrrt of the phone jolts me as if I had touched a downed tram cable.

"Grass Gott! Haus 3a."

I must breathe. Why can't I breathe? Blessed God, I'm scared.

"Is Peter there?" A pretty, feminine voice with a rolling Bavarian accent breaks through the blinding haze of pain, yanking me back into the world around me.

"Ein Moment, bitte. Let me check."

Searing pain tears me back inside myself. God, why can't I breathe?

"Michael? Are you all right?" I recognize the telephone caller's voice as it wins another round in a hideous game of tug-of-war.

"I'll be all right, Uschi. Let me me get...never mind, here he is."

I look up to see that Peter and most of my housemates are there. I must have cried out. Silly of me. I ought get used to the pain. It will soon be all I have left because I will not take pain killers and fry my brains. My housemates are hovering over me, concerned, scared, caring. Hey! Why am I lying on the floor trying to crack the telephone receiver?

"The phone is for you, Peter, it's Uschi."

"Mein Gott, Michael! Are you okay...what?...oh, thank you...hallo? Uschi, gruass di. Wie geht's?...jo, mai, des hoab i aa gedoacht...do ned..." I like the sound of Bavarian. Plump, lilting, soft.

A friendly voice--I am in such pain that I cannot identify it--speaks gently to me: "Michael? Are you all right? Come, let's get you back to your room."

I am floating. The pain is burning me alive. I want to sleep. I want never to wake up. No, I am asleep and this is just a bad dream and I am going to wake up and all this never happened. Oh, why won't the phone ring for me?

Another unidentifiable voice seeps in through the pain: "Michael, it is all right. We are right here. What can we do for you? Michael? MICHAEL!" The voice melts away from the pain's heat as someone begins shaking me.

Why is someone shaking me? Who is that screaming? Oh my God, I'm the one screaming! I am floating on an ocean and the waves are

47

made of pain. The pain rises and falls, washing over me like a North Sea storm. Ride the storm. Rise and fall with the waves. Drift on this endless sea. Breathe.

"Uli, get a towel! Bernhard, hold his shoulders down!" Mona is going to be a doctor. Mona is my friend. God, I need my friends. "Michael, can you hear me?"

Why isn't the phone ringing for me?

Outer reality bursts in as someone puts a cold towel on my forehead.

Maybe if someone put a bullet through my head instead. Yes. That's it. Shoot me. Use a large calibre gun. .44 Magnum. Just don't miss. Breathe. That's it. Breathe. Stay calm. No, don't shoot me. I ...don't...want...to...die.

"*Domino, misere* me..."

"I think he's feeling better...he's speaking Latin," Eberhard quips. He is trying to cheer us up. He is my friend. I need him.

"Michael, I am going to call the hospital for you. This is getting ridiculous." Mona's face is so grim. I wonder if all my doctors will be so grim. Is it really that grim? Please, I don't want to die.

I think Uli is crying. Silently, tears are coursing down her face as she wipes mine free of sweat. She is smiling faintly. I don't want to see my friends suffer.

Please, ring.

November 4, 1980

Bernhard tells me that they took turns staying with me because this went on all night. Someone carried Uli to her room after she fell asleep in a corner, still sitting upright. I can't remember who it was, but someone has brought me breakfast in bed. I ask that my breakfast be moved to the dining room because I am going to get bedside service enough. We laugh. We are laughing at everything. God, we must all be really scared. Why are they scared? I'm the one who is going to die, whose body is eating him alive. Maybe they are afraid to die, just like I am, and my impending demise reminds them of their own mortality. We are in our twenties. Who thinks of dying when you are in your twenties?

"Michael?"

God! Where do these voices keep coming from?

The pain is starting again.

Why doesn't the phone ring?

My friends are carrying me back to my room. Someone is holding down my shoulders, someone else is holding down my hips.

Breathe. Stay calm. Just ride the rise and fall of the pain. But, it isn't falling.

Someone is pressing a cold towel to my forehead and I can feel the steam coming off it. I am burning up. My leg is trying to murder me. I think it is succeeding.

Breathe. Why doesn't the phone ring for me?

When the seizure ends, I notice everyone is soaked in sweat. I can't believe this, but I am asking why. Mona tells me this episode lasted twenty minutes.

"The hospital was trying to make emergency space for you when I called yesterday."

"Thank you for trying." Mona is one hell of a friend.

Please, ring.

It is much later in the afternoon. I think I have been sleeping, but, then again, I may have been hallucinating. The pain is incredible. Every time I think, "This is it. It cannot get worse," I find out something new about the human capacity for pain. Why do I have this sickening feeling that I will be discovering a lot about how much pain I can experience? I do not think I like this very much. God, I have to pee. This is ridiculous. I am being eaten alive, burning with horrid pain, and I have to pee. I start to laugh. Do my friends think I have gone crazy? I sure hope not because I need my friends. They help me to the bathroom. It feels good to pee. I am watching this just like one watches a movie. This isn't really happening to me. I think I am becoming delirious.

Brrrrrt-brrrrrt! I jump out of my skin.

"Michael?" yet another faceless voice calls. I drag myself along the wall before my friends can grab me.

"This is the Orthopedic Clinic of the Klinikum rechts der Isar. We have a bed for you. Come in as soon as possible. Do you have a ride or shall we send an ambulance?"

50

The phone. It rang. My call. God...

"Michael? Are you there?"

"Yes, thank you. A friend will drive me." I hang up. That was it. I have burned with pain and fear and delirium for three days, just for ten god-damn seconds on the phone--and all that is yet to come.

I dial. Hans-Joachim answers. My best friend. My brother in spirit. I need him.

"Hans-Joachim? Michael. It's time." We hang up. Germans are very efficient.

I'm scared. Try to breathe. Stay calm. God help me. I don't want this. It isn't happening. Breathe. I...don't...want...to...die...Just breathe. My bags are packed. I did that three days ago.

Michael bore the truth of his healing, his transcendence, at the intersection of now *and* then...

Chapter 9 The Reflecting Pool

April 29, 1992

Most of my head lies in a shopping bag next to my bed. What else was there to do? When I sat up this morning, much of my hair did not, so I spent the next half hour pulling my hair out--literally. Right now, what is left of it is cropped short, waiting until I have the energy to shave off the remainder.

It is hard not to reflect back twelve year ago to when my hair fell out from my first chemotherapy. My hair hung in long, spiraling curls down to my shoulders. The Munichites called me Tilly, after the 30 Years War general in Electoral Bavarian service. I was sick at heart to have my hair fall out and left mats of it in place, anchored to my scalp by a few hold-outs against the fallout. A hat held the mess down and concealed the hideous truth from the rest of the world.

One bus ride changed that. Normally, Germans don't, won't make disparaging comments in public, but one elderly lady made it clear she found long hair utterly disgusting. There was the sound of much air being swallowed. Germans often gulp a bit of air like Americans "uh-huh", especially to stifle the utterance of nasty comments. My response was a bit more brutal. I simply wheeled about, doffed my hat and, grabbing a mat, ripped it from my head.

"There, madam. Since it disturbs you so, and since I may be dying of this cancer I have and have no further use of hair, I shall simply remove that which offends you."

The fury helped define my life and felt so good.

This morning, shaving my head was simply something else to do, just another part of the process. No anger, no remorse, no misery. It was curious, however, that my hair hung down in spiraling curls almost to my shoulders, just like twelve years ago. I had chosen to grow it out again after all these years, as well as maintaining a Cavalier moustache and beard, all to wear my love of the early 17th century on my head (instead of my sleeve). Just like twelve years ago.

A few days before the present diagnosis, my sister, Cheryl, had sent me a picture taken after I returned to the United States in 1981. I had been off chemotherapy long enough to get some fuzz on my pate and a goatee on my face. It was a chilling sensation that coursed through my body as I looked at the picture, which was like some dark omen pulled from a deck of magic cards in a sinister fortune teller's parlor. It spurred me to think back, my mind covering twelve years and thousands of miles in an instant, in a lifetime.

I had just had my knee replaced and had been pumped full of chemotherapy. My walk was reduced from the swordsman's precise, purposeful gait to a lamed, shuffling hobble. My mind returns to the present, snapped back as if a rubber band stretched too tautly. My prosthesis had just been replaced last August in Germany and now I am back in the U.S. being pumped full of chemotherapy, my swordsman's ballet again seeing another curtain fall.

So many other things bounce me between here and there and now and then, like a great matrix with a myriad of connections, some tenuous, some tenacious, with me in the middle being all things, for I am the matrix of my memories and experiences.

Connections. Parallels. Relationships. Places. Time.

Now cancer is simply part of my journey through life, and since I savor that life, and especially that journey, I shall savor too my cancer.

Here, although America has continued to be a land that shows me a face of cruelty, it is where I live, where my friends and family live and what I am, together with their love and support, makes this place more real and useful than paradise. This place is home.

A dozen year ago, I composed piece of music after piece of music in a desperate attempt to express my love for a woman now long since departed from my life. Now, I compose music because it expresses my love of being, and while there is no woman currently as my intimate companion in love, there is no desperation to find and secure such a person. Such a relationship will occur when it will and ought. I have no reason to be desperate for love, especially when my life is so full.

Still, as twelve years ago, there is often terrible pain and I am so weak that getting out of bed is my daily triumph. But much has changed in medicine in twelve years. Back then, my veins were systematically converted to steel draught. Now, I have a low maintenance catheter in my chest that will, if my luck is good, stay with me throughout my treatments (odd to think that my life is six inches long...). Back then, anything, everything made me retch my guts out, and that year of nausea and vomiting was well the worst aspect of the ordeal, at least, physically. Now there is a new wonder drug and I have not had more than a few inklings of that horror, and a day or two of acid indigestion is hardly even worth a raised eyebrow (I can still do that --they haven't fallen out yet...). My new prosthetic knee is the best that world-leading German prosthetics can provide, in part because my 20 hours a week of fencing and kendo helped redefine the uses, limitations, and design considerations of such devices. New chemotherapies have led to quantum leaps forward in successful treatment, whereas my form of cancer twelve years ago was an almost certain trip to the grave.

All things change. I did. Twelve years ago, most everything was negative. Now, I am on the positive end of the magnet.

In rereading my writings and listening to my conversations, the recurring theme is complete healing. The first time I had cancer, I cherished my suffering because it defined my life, made things clear to me, gave me an ill sense of purpose, and a sense of tragic heroism. More ominously, it confirmed the terrible lessons of my childhood; namely, that if I was suffering so much, I must truly be a bad person, unworthy of success, be it materially or spiritually. True, I learned to be strong, to persevere, and I did learn a great deal about spiritual growth. Moreover, much good came of it and I did become happier. Still, I could not accept that I deserved success and love. The latent pain was, twelve years later, still too great for me to truly open my heart all the way and let others in. I could give--after a fashion--but I could not receive. Half a healing is actually no healing at all.

Today, my life is lived moment by moment, openly and as fully as possible. It was a great agony to open my heart because the pain leapt out like a ravaging beast, but once it was loose, it was gone, replaced by the love of friends and family. Asking myself the dread question, "how do you want to live out your possibly final days?", I found I no longer wished to suffer in matters within my control. If my tumor aches badly, I take a painkiller. If I don't feel well, I go to bed and either sleep or meditate. I affirm with all my being that I can be blissful, serene, and happy, and I am.

My oncologist said that I most likely missed my chance to be cured twelve years ago, and although I will most assuredly beat this cancer, I will probably face it again in five years. And again. And again. I may only have ten years left, to be a corpse at age 45. On the other hand I could live to age 70. Or, I could be run over by an apple cart. Who cares? Live now, fully, or you are not completely alive. Since I will be dead soon enough (like all of us), I chose to be absolutely alive--and enjoy it. Half a healing will not do this time around and even if, for whatever reason, my body dies, the rest of me will die healed, die as a human being who has answered all significant questions in his life.

56

Chapter 10 Harper

May 17, 1992

Author's note: the names in this chapter have been changed.

Languorously, the bed tumbles away from me like a satellite pushed from its steady orbit. I follow it on its journey, pressing myself deeper into a receding mattress, all to a soft thrumming sound that comes from nowhere, goes nowhere, least of all away. Part of my fragmented consciousness tells me this is just a post-chemotherapy hallucination, another conveys awed wonder for the journey, another trembles in terror at a thing beyond reason or control.

I have been on many such journeys, given my long years of struggle with cancer, so I just press myself a little deeper into the mattress and try to relax, letting the process run its course: all things end, I remind myself. This is no different, as processes go. Only the specific details of the individual episodes change.

Suddenly, I am not alone. Near the foot of my free-falling bed is a woman in silver-gold samite. She is all women, now fair and blonde, now the colors of midnight, ever-changing, but constantly anima. I marvel, despite the waves of vertigo. Equally suddenly, she has a harp in her lap and the slightest touch of ever-changing fingers brings forth music beyond description. My soul soars and rides the music like cosmic carnival. It is glorious. I am glorious. Who cares if it is a post-chemotherapy hallucination. Pure anima, pure music, pure bliss. My bed can tumble into oblivion for all I care.

Something goes *click* in my brain and I find myself looking at an illumination in 14th Century style my friend, Lori, made for me over four years ago. Lori is dead, killed by a second occurrence of cancer and a shattering despair. Something else goes *click* in my brain and I realize this is the fourth anniversary of Lori's rapid journey into death. *Click-click-click-click*, like a prison at evening lockup, a prison whose locks and bars are inescapable memories. Terror, panic, and claustrophobia seize me. I fight back, clinging to reason and the music. Then, time and space rip apart, right before my eyes. Everything and everytime happen all at once. Overwhelmed, I press myself yet deeper into my tumbling bed, seeking slim comfort in the tangible, but the living past becomes part of the living now like two movies playing simultaneously on one screen.

Lori is lying in her bed, having just undergone abdominal surgery. I see, hear, feel as if I were going through it again. Hell, I am going through it again. Lori, my friend and fellow cancer survivor, the only being with whom I can share all of my feelings about having gone through cancer and have every word, every gesture, every feeling, every silence truly understood. Lori, my friend and fellow history buff, with

58

whom I can hold endless discourses on ancient arcana. Lori, my friend and fellow musician, with whom I can share all the poignantly, artfully wrought sounds of times gone by. Oh Lori, if I could take this from you, but we know I--no one--truly can.

I am in fencing gear, having just given a private lesson, my clavichord under my right arm, music in a blue nylon pouch slung over my other shoulder. I march right into the hospital. Visiting hours are over. Fuck 'em, this isn't a visit. No one stops me as I head for Lori's room. Up against the wall lies a gurney, so I avail myself of it, and placing the clavichord on it, I continue my unstoppable march. I snag an adjustable chair from the Nurses' Station. No one says or does anything. I cannot see my face for I am looking out of eyes that saw four years ago, but my face must be a study in terrifying resolve. No one looks at me, seeks out my gaze. I march on, enter Lori's room, and start setting up. The room opens to the left of the door, the bed in which Lori is painfully lying is against that far left wall.

"I'm not going to be much company--haven't slept in thirty-six hours," Lori gasps as waves of abdominal cramps batter her.

"Who said I was here for the company?" I blandly shoot back, pushing the gurney against the wall across from the door, windows affording a glorious view of drab medical buildings and scattered parking lots. My hand finds a height lever and I adjust the gurney to "playing height". The chair is rapidly brought to a comfortable position, so I settle in. I start playing her favorite pieces from the 16th and 17th centuries, ones well practiced and loved.

Lori sighs, then falls asleep. I keep playing and playing and playing. The sky turns indigo, then black. I keep playing and playing. Lori sleeps, a smile gracing her face. I run out of music I know or can play. Still, I keep playing and playing, the muses pouring music into me. Six hours go by and finally I stop because I am spent in every conceivable way. I thank God I am a musician.

"Thank you." Lori awoke the instant I stopped.

"You're welcome. Sleep well." I pack my things and go.

Reality, if reality it is, skips ahead three months to August 1988. Lori is dying and it is a matter of days now (then). Her crazed mother, claiming she alone should take care of her daughter, had all but isolated Lori. No one goes through cancer alone. To have to even try--God, my whole being shudders in remembering how I felt as I boarded that plane in Munich, in 1981, to leave my home and friends, my support network and source of strength and comfort. But to actually be alone with the pain, alone in pain, in terror, and only inanimate walls to hear the tears and screams as your body eats itself. Now, I cannot stop shaking as I feel Lori's despair, isolation, and pain. Once a week visits and frequent phone calls from one person are not enough.

There was her friend, Jon, who had quit his job to take care of her, but Lori's mother had gotten a court order restraining him from seeing her (how Lori's mother pulled it off, I have no idea--damn her and the court that issued the order!). Lori's voice on the phone is no more than anguished sobs and bitter disconsolation and I have no words of comfort, for none are left to be had.

Lori died that night--alone.

Everything fades, fuses, and abruptly I am in the present now--alone. I am shaking, clinging to a bed still tumbling through space, but, thank God, not time. And then it hits me, how I had played for Lori and brought her peace, but who would play for me?

I scream out my plea, "who will play for me?" My only answer is my own sobbing voice. The harper is gone.

I will not die tonight--not alone or otherwise. This is just a process, the passage through a moment's terror, a moment's worth of memories, a moment's hallucination, or whatever the hell you want to call it. I have no names, no descriptions, just some time to bide. It will pass. All things do--and therein are the kernels of comfort, comfort Lori hardly had, comfort my friends and family give me in abundance.

Lori's mother never told me when or where Lori was to be buried, hiding her away even in death, so I never got to say farewell. She had so wanted to learn to play the harp.

Farewell, my friend.

Chapter 11 Friend of Mine

I desperately wanted to answer Michael's cry, "Who will play for me?" Without hesitating, I promised to bring someone for him when he read *Harper* to me over the phone in May.

"Someone to play and play and play," I said, wanting to soothe his fear of dying alone.

"Thank you," he cried.

I would come through on this, I could feel it, yet whom to bring and how was unknown to me.

During our first visit at the end of April, I told him how I had made arrangements to leave at any time for however long to be with him. So far, he really wanted me to proceed with my daily life, telling me that if things started to get bad that he would call for me. *Harper* told me that while he was doing well so far, nightly phone calls and monthly visits were not going to be enough. My daily life could wait.

I also remembered our hug goodbye in April. I could still feel it. Michael's embrace was as strong as ever, but I knew as I held him that his body was so sick. How many more hugs would we be blessed with?

There was a lifetime in that hug for both of us. Now, having listened to *Harper*, I looked ahead and prepared myself for going to Portland.

"Do whatever is needful," he told me in his upbeat, supportive voice, meaning be flexible and open to whatever arises.

Along with my friend, Beth, I had already purchased roundtrip air tickets to Portland for a week in June, scheduled to arrive on the 12th, the day of Michael's release from another round of chemo at St. Vincent. Upon my return to the Bay Area on the 19th, I would pack my things and drive back to Portland with Beth's Nissan Sentra. Michael had told me that he could not get into my Toyota truck. I was happy that I would be able to provide him with comfortable transportation.

Beth, a classical musician, readily agreed to play her French horn for Michael. She prepared a concert of works by Mozart and Bach. Still, she and I both knew that one "gig" would not really answer Michael's cry, *who will play for me?* Who, we wondered, would be there for him to share every word, every gesture, every feeling, every silence? Who would be his harper?

June 9 was my twenty-ninth birthday. For the first time since I was six years old, I wanted a party. I felt a need to have all of my friends around me, partly for the gathering of support, mostly to say goodbye for the duration--whatever that would be. Together with my friend, Melissa, whose birthday is a few days after mine, we had a double Gemini birthday party on the 11th. The surprise was that everyone showed up. The house was packed with friends offering me *Calvin and Hobbes* books, the only thing I could think of when people asked what to give me.

One friend gave me nothing. Clairemarie, my closest friend for nearly a decade, often mistaken for my sister even though she towers over me at five-foot-seven.

"Heidi, I'm sorry. I went to so many stores. I looked at so many different things, but nothing felt right. I've never had trouble finding a gift for you. Why can't I find something for you?"

"Because what I want is something that I probably can't have, so giving me nothing is really an honest present."

"You want Michael to be healed."

"Yes."

"No wonder I couldn't find anything for you in the stores." She gave me a teary look and hugged me.

As more people arrived, Clairemarie sat down in the kitchen with a plate of food and an audience of begging pets.

"I want to spend the summer, at least, with Michael," I said. "Everything else is going on hold."

"Absolutely. Anytime anybody is that sick, you just have to go."

"I'm nervous about it. I don't want him to feel like I'm in the way, but I want to work on our book together and I feel that nothing else matters as much as being with him. It's hard because I know that he's sensitive about disrupting my life. And it's hard because I don't know how to make this work financially for very long, especially if he goes back to Munich at the end of the summer if the treatments here don't work. If, if, if."

"It's definitely right to go. You don't want to look back on this time and feel like you missed out on being with him. Don't worry."

"Thanks," I said, grateful for her reassurance. "Would you like to read some of the things Michael has written for the book?"

"Yeah, sure."

I brought her *2:44 a.m.* and *Reflecting Pool.*

"In all the years we've known each other, you've never met him," I said.

"It's just never worked out, Heid."

They had missed each other several times. Whenever Michael had come to the Bay Area to see me, Clairemarie was out of town or out of the country. Whenever Clairemarie had gone to Oregon with me, Michael was out of town or out of the country. He was even in her house once--while she was in India.

"Now you can meet Michael through his writing." I handed her the envelope with the stories, handwritten in Michael's unique, flowing script, a type of Old World European calligraphy that he had fashioned into his own style and signature.

And that was the last I heard from Clairemarie for the rest of the night. She did not move from her chair, holding Michael's writings for hours.

Happy with my library of *Calvin and Hobbes*, the house now empty of friends, I went over to Clairemarie.

"Heidi, I'm in love with your brother."

"I told you, his writing is really wonderful."

65

"It's not just his writing. It's *him.* It's like he jumped out of the envelope. His heart is so noble. He has such a grand spirit. I'm in love with him."

"Oh, God."

"Oh, Heidi."

"You mean that after knowing me for so long and never meeting him and never being very interested in him personally, tonight there's this opening?"

"I'm telling you, it's like he jumped out of the envelope."

"Well, I'm going to see him tomorrow. I'll tell him that you love him."

"Oh, no, don't tell him that," she said, shocked.

"Why not?" How naive could I be?

"He doesn't know me. We've never met. Don't you think it would be really unbelievable and awkward? *Oh, Michael, Heidi gave me your stories and now I'm in love with you...*"

"No. He knows you through me. You know him through me. We all know each other."

"But, Heidi, now I'm in love with him. Maybe he won't want anything to do with me."

"I doubt that. I'm sure he'd like to meet you."

"I wouldn't want to intrude on him. He has so much to deal with already."

"Let me talk to him. You can come see us this summer."

Clairemarie groaned, fidgeted.

"I'll talk to him."

"Oh, all right, but *don't* tell him I'm in love with him."

"I think you two have a lot in common," I persisted.

"Oh, please."

I loaned Clairemarie three tapes of Michael's music, so that she could hear more of his talent and, I hoped, be convinced to meet him. I held his music in the palm of my hand and looked at her.

"Clairemarie."

"What?"

"Clairemarie," I said again, a chill running down my spine.

"*What?*"

"Clairemarie, you're a *harper.*"

"So?"

"You'll see. I hope you'll see."

Beth and I left for Portland the next morning. I was so excited to see Michael that I rushed out of the elevator at St. Vincent, ran down the hall and into his room, arms wide open.

I stood holding the air. The room was empty.

"Where is he?" I said, baffled. I looked around.

"Beth?" No answer.

"Beth? Where are you? Where is everybody?"

I heard voices and laughter coming from the room next door. I walked over to the room, feeling foolish that in my haste I had run right by Michael. Beth peered into the room, amused, while Michael casually leaned on his walking stick, talking about condoms and safe sex with a female patient. His dark blue Stetson fedora added a dapper touch to his features.

"You take care, Chrissie," he said and turned to greet Beth and me. Chrissie would later show up in Michael's hospital room telling ribald jokes.

"That Bleomycin really nailed me to the wall," Michael strode out of St. Vincent, shaking his finger.

"Sounds like a pretty rough week," Beth said sympathetically.

"M-hm."

Michael's chemotherapy protocol had just been changed from Adriamycin and Ifosfamide to Cisplatin, Etoposide and Bleomycin because a recent CAT scan showed that the main tumor in his pelvis had grown slightly larger, although the metastatic rate was down.

"What exactly," he had asked his doctors, "does this mean?"

"Technically, you should be dead."

Now, Michael lead us out of the hospital, his body yet to reveal the outcome of the new arsenal of drugs.

"How's your chest feel since they drained those two liters of fluid from your lung?" I asked.

"Not too bad. They drained two-point-oh-six liters." Michael accounted for every unit, not about to round off the severity of what he had been through.

"You know, Michael, you look really good clean shaven, even if you lost your hair to chemo not a razor."

He gave me a big smile, "It's the only way I shave."

We went to lunch at the deli near his house. Michael's appetite was strong, but by the end of lunch he needed to rest. He and Beth planned her concert for the next day, Saturday.

Michael called for me in the evening. The taste of Cisplatin, which he always called the Taste of Hell, terrified him of cancer twelve years ago and of cancer now.

"Just talk to me," his voice shook.

I covered everything from the weather to what courage he had.

"You're helping," he said, beginning to relax. "The Taste of Hell has given me something else to write about, too." Michael gave a long sigh, ready for a night's rest after more than a moment's terror.

Beth's concert never happened. Saturday morning, June 13, Michael's right lung collapsed and we took him back to St. Vincent.

I could not understand why he had been released from the hospital in the first place when the hospital knew that he was at increased risk for a collapsed lung after a thoracentesis. But that is how the system worked. By the time Michael was back in the same room, twenty-four hours later, three people had occupied that room.

In the evening, Michael underwent the placement of two tubes into his chest to siphon off the air and fluid leaking out of his lung. The placement of these tubes is brutal to undergo, but Michael's nurse told me how calm he remained. She expressed her amazement at his capacity for pain. He expressed his amazement at her capacity for pain since it was her hand that he had gripped.

69

Michael and Beth visited in his room, in lieu of her concert, and discovered a mutual love of Bavaria and Monty Python. They launched into renditions of their favorite Monty Python scenes, especially the part about the budgies. Michael also took the opportunity to invoke the line most appropriate to his cancerous condition, a line which he said whenever people asked him how he was: *I'm not dead yet.* Michael and Beth left Mozart and Bach in the dust.

I put off talking to him about Clairemarie for three days. Then, in the intimate setting of a hospital room, I said, "My friend, Clairemarie, read *2:44 a.m.* and *Reflecting Pool.* She really loved them."

"That's wonderful."

"She'd like to meet you if that's o'kay. She's really very moved by you."

"Well, it would be nice to meet her after all this time."

"I mean, she really likes you."

"Oh?" Michael gave me a pointed look.

"Oh." I looked away.

"She plays the harp."

"Ooh."

"It's a monarch concert grand pedal harp that was used in the Portland Symphony."

"Oh! I know that harp!" If he could have, he would have jumped up and down on the bed.

To Michael, knowing Clairemarie's harp was a way of knowing her. This harp is the only one of its kind, fashioned in glossy ebony and gold.

70

Standing six-foot-three, it is exquisitely beautiful to hear and see. Ebony and gold like Michael's vision in *Harper...now fair and blonde, now the colors of midnight...*

Michael kept looking at me. "You know what I say. My friends are your friends."

"And my friends are your friends."

We gave each other a silly handshake, recognizing the importance of what we just said.

Clairemarie called me the next night.

"Heidi, I don't know how to arrange all of this, but I'm thinking to come see Michael."

"That's great! He'd like to meet you. I talked to him about you. He knows your harp."

"He does? How does he know my harp?"

"From the Portland Symphony."

"Oh, my God."

"So you want to come?"

"I think so." She added directly, "I know how seriously ill Michael is. I know that I cannot play with this or treat him in any kind of superficial way. There is no time for that."

"Clairemarie, he wants to meet you and I know you well enough to say that you'll respect him and the condition he's in. You already do."

"I just don't want to add anything more to what he already has to deal with."

71

"I don't think you will. If anything, your meeting him will help. He *wants* to meet you. You can drive back to Portland with me when I come home to get my stuff."

"When are you going back to Portland?"

"I get home on the nineteenth and I want to be back here within a few days."

"I'll have to make arrangements with work. The more notice I can give them the better."

"Well, let's see how it goes between now and then. I'd love your company on the drive. It takes about eleven hours to get to Portland."

"All right."

"So you'll do it? You'll come back with me?"

"Yes."

When I got home to the Bay Area, Michael was still in the hospital. Clairemarie had arranged to leave her health food store job for a week at the end of June. So, our travel plans were set. We would go to Portland on June 30. At the end of one week, Clairemarie and I would drive to Mt. Shasta City, about midway between Portland and the Bay Area, to meet Beth. Clairemarie and Beth would return to the Bay Area and I would go back to Portland.

Clairemarie was at my house one evening when I was ready to make my nightly call to Michael at the hospital.

"Want to talk to Michael?" I teased her.

"I'd be too shy," she pushed herself further into the chair.

I got on the phone with Michael and he started by asking about Clairemarie.

"She's here at the house."

"I want to talk to her."

I put the phone down and went back to Clairemarie, still burrowed in the chair.

"He wants to talk to you," I said as she remained glued in place.

"I'm too shy."

I reasoned with her.

"I'm too shy."

I pleaded with her.

"I'm too shy."

Then I grabbed her with all my might and dragged her to the phone.

"Michael, here's Clairemarie. Sorry for the wait."

I shoved the phone in her hand.

"So, after all this time, we *finally* meet!" Michael boomed.

Their rapport was immediate, made profound by Michael's first statement after their introduction.

"I would go through this cancer a hundred times if it would heal one heart."

They had an immediate good time, too, as a combination of playfulness and the profound came to typify their relationship. Clairemarie giggled and screamed over the phone for two hours.

"You sound so vital. I can't believe you're in the hospital. Are you sure you have lung cancer? Don't you need to come up for air?" She would say when Michael made one of his infrequent pauses. Then more giggles.

Beth and I looked at each other often and cracked up.

"That was hard," I said.

"Do you think they'll get off the phone?"

"Maybe by the time Michael leaves St. Vincent."

Clairemarie finally handed the phone back to me.

"When you two come here," he said in a conspiratorial whisper, "bring a padlock."

"A padlock?" I repeated. Clairemarie started madly kissing my neck. "Michael, she's *kissing me*. I think these are for you."

"Of course they're for me!"

"Why a padlock?"

"I won't tell."

"I won't either," Clairemarie said between kisses.

That is what I got for my efforts to bring them together. Their first conversation ended with me smothered in kisses.

Michael got out of the hospital on June 23, having spent almost all of the month to date at St. Vincent. He called me from his home and wanted to talk to Clairemarie again.

"I know she wants to talk to you, too," I said, "but she's too shy to call."

"Well, I'm not shy! Give me her phone number."

I promptly got off the phone. When he called Clairemarie, he got her answering machine and left the following message in true Monty

74

Python spirit, "Hello, Clairemarie, these are the still mortal remains of Michael..." No man had ever given her a line like that and she wasted no time calling him back.

Until Clairemarie and I left for Portland, I rarely got through to her or to Michael. So much for being shy.

But Michael called me Friday, June 26.

"Capital Neep Day!" His happy voice resonated over the phone.

He was pain free. *Pain free.* Without any medical intervention beyond a massage, his body was spontaneously set free from every pain that ailed it--cancer, recovery from pneumothorax, a debilitated prosthetic leg.

"I'm a survivor for the second time," he praised himself, astonished.

Spontaneous remission. I dared to hope for that. I knew that spontaneous remissions happened to people, that if anyone was capable of it, Michael certainly was. *I'm a survivor for the second time.*

His pain free state began that day during a session with his massage therapist, Holly. As in every session since the recurrence, she felt two major blocks of energy in Michael's body at the locations of the tumors-- in his chest, in his pelvis. But something different happened during this particular massage as she held her hands on Michael's back, over his lungs. Holly was knocked off her feet, landing on top of Michael while they both visualized releasing the cancer. He said that if he had not already been lying down that he would have been knocked off his feet, too. In all of their work together, which spanned four years, neither one of them had ever felt such an explosive release of energy.

75

When Holly recovered herself, she touched Michael's chest and hip again. No blocks. Michael got up from that massage a renewed man, pain free, breathing deeply with ease.

"Right before I called you, Heidi, I *thanked* the tumor. I *thanked* it for everything it has taught me. I *thanked* it for helping me understand how many people love me. I *thanked* it for opening my heart to myself and others. I *thanked* it for healing my relationship with the American medical community. I *thanked* it for teaching me to be a true warrior, for taking me beyond the path of greater pain. *I thanked it and I let it go.*" He spoke with clarity, ecstatic.

"Michael, I thank you."

"Heidi, there's more. After I thanked the tumor, I got up and could do my Chi Kung breathing exercises again. That has been *impossible* for me since my lung collapsed. I got up, lifted my arms high above my head, put my palms together and as I inhaled deeply and slowly, I pulled my arms down to my belly, and then exhaled, slowly, pushing my arms straight in front of me. I did this not just once but over and over. Just like before! And I haven't even coughed *once*."

"And there's more," he hurried on, exuberant. "I was sitting down-- without pain--and heard my cane start to slide off the back of the chair. I leapt up, spun around, and grabbed my cane before it hit the ground. I haven't been able to move like that for months. I feel like I can fence again!"

Michael maintained this state of freedom for nine hours. Gradually, over the next two days, his health diminished until he felt again like God

76

had stepped on him. But the boost to his body, however transitory, and the boost to our morale remained as a shining example that the impossible *is* possible. We kept that faith. *I'm a survivor for the second time.*

Michael could hardly wait to meet Clairemarie. Also, because she had sworn over the phone to plant red kisses all over his head, he prepared himself well for her arrival. The moment she came through the door, he walked up to her, did not say hello, and pointed to his forehead.

Clairemarie bent forward to see a strip of masking tape labeled, *peel and kiss.*

She gently followed the instructions while Michael giggled away. He wore that big red kiss like a badge of honor for the rest of the day.

Seeing Michael, I could not fathom what effort it must have been for him to take care of himself during the week between his release from the hospital and our arrival. His movements were more restricted than ever, he was weak and more painful. His right leg was in a brace because, during his long hospitalization, his muscles had atrophied around the prosthesis and it would otherwise fall apart. He could barely put on his own socks. Plus, Portland was *hot.* Michael wilted in the heat, especially when ill, and his house had no air conditioning. I regretted that we had not come to him sooner. His loss of vitality was new to him, so new that only with our arrival did he begin to realize that he required help far beyond what he could provide for himself. If we were to see anymore "Capital Neep Days" then Clairemarie and I had to get to work. Fast.

She helped Michael upstairs to his room, to their first moment alone. As soon as he was in bed, he reached out for Clairemarie with both arms and pulled her to his chest, holding her tightly, crying.

"I can't do this alone anymore."

"You won't have to. I'll stay. I'll stay for as long as you need me. If you want to live, I'll help you live and if you die, Michael, I'll help you die."

"I want to live."

"I will stay and I will help you live."

Clairemarie's spontaneous promise, made that first day with Michael, formed an undying commitment to him. Whatever obligations she had in California would all be put on hold. She gave Michael her word and she lived by it with the conviction that he, too, would live.

"My healing began the day Heidi and Clairemarie got here," he would say repeatedly.

Clairemarie started taking care of Michael the first day by cooking, making his bed and making sure that he stayed in it to rest, and bathing him. Reluctantly, he let her wash his forehead.

She bathed him respectfully, kneeling behind him, hesitant to remove his pajama bottoms.

"Michael, do you...do you want me to wash...you know...all of you?"

Perhaps she had done too much too soon to rally his strength because Michael whipped around in a burst of energy and snatched the washcloth from her hand. With a lecherous grin, eyes rolling, he gyrated like he was masturbating to the moon.

Well scrubbed, he handed the washcloth back to Clairemarie who sat in shock.

"I only did that as a joke, you know," he said as if she needed the reassurance.

"I know."

Clean, fed, and rested Michael sat propped in bed and received a large giftwrapped box from Clairemarie, addressed to, "Sir Michael." When someone had asked her if he really was a Lord, she said, "He is to me."

The first gift he pulled out of the box was "Lady Bear".

"Oh!" He was six years old again, squeezing this very soft, white teddy bear. "Oh! Oh!"

"Oh, look at her dress and the *lace*," he looked at Lady Bear from all angles, admiring the floral patterned clothes Clairemarie had made. Lady Bear's white cottontail stuck out from the backside of her dress.

"Oh! Look at her pearl drop baroque earrings! I just love these," he gushed.

After a few minutes he switched back to being a real mature guy, his voice an octave lower.

"Heidi, put the bear on that stand against the wall."

"Don't you want Lady Bear in bed with you?"

"Put her over there."

"But she's the softest of soft bears. You can sleep with her. She'll keep you company."

"Here." He held Lady Bear at arms length.

79

I slowly took her and put her on the stand, but then I grabbed Lady Bear and held her high above my head. I pointed at Michael.

"You'll never be healed until you can love this bear!"

Michael spent the night with Lady Bear, although he pretended not to notice her. Without pretense, however, he did notice another gift from Clairemarie, an ornate handmade box of green marbled paper with a lavender rose on the lid and a gold baroque latch set with drops of frosted glass. Inside were dozens of small pastel candles and one white candle with gold stars. Each candle had a wish attached to it. Clairemarie had spent days writing these wishes during breaks at work, on BART trains, in her kitchen late into the night. Here is a sample of these lights for Michael, some whimsical, some passionate and lewd, some transcendent, all given from the heart:

A Very Large Wish--
To share a Dance with you--
if but just Once...!!!

Oh Heart of Wisdom--
Yet another Wish--
That your Laughter Born
of tears Rise above this Earth
and Reach to the very Halls of
the Gods of Life and Death. And
with that Sword pierce Them

to Their Very Core...

A Wish to be able to
spend a Long Night with
you Playing Music For
the Moon.

A Wish Far Into a Quiet Night--
That You Delight in
the Truth that you are
Loved so very much.

A Wish--That the Refinement
of Spirit that you embody be
known by many...

A Wish Born out of Deep
Consideration and True Lust--
If we are going to die
anyway, wouldn't it be
wonderful to do it while making
Mad Passionate Love.

A somewhat Oral Wish--
To slowly feed you

half-melted strawberry
ice cream in the
Candle Light.

A Wish to hear you
laugh so hard you cry:

The unique candle, white with gold stars, based on a Sufi saying:

A Wishful Thought--
Perhaps Eternity is Now,
The Future Is Now. No past,
or present or future as separate
periods of time--All is within
the soul's embrace Now which
is Your Future. Live Today
and Your Future can hold
Nothing but Joy!!

And a wish that came true:

A Wish...or perhaps a
Living Poem--
That we shall never
share a Farewell because

we have found a Home in
each others' Heart.

Michael's response to Clairemarie for the wish candles became a repeated warning. During chemotherapy or fits of pain or coughing or when he seemed to be sound asleep, Michael would suddenly pop one eye open and mischieviously say, "I'm going to get you for those candles." His teasing was an anchor to the future.

Michael rallied quickly, but within just a few days of my arrival, I was overwhelmed by the amount of care that he needed. I was also the only person in the house on a day schedule. I was used to going to bed by 11 p.m. and getting up before 6 a.m.. Most of my work days required me to be on the job by 6:30 a.m. to care for the hospitalized animals and emergencies. Michael and Clairemarie were night owls and when they were revving up, I was winding down. When they were going to bed, I was getting up. I had a difficult time at best adapting to a reversed body clock. I also did not have the ability to be roused from sleep if Michael coughed or stirred in the next room, but Clairemarie would run to him before her eyes were even fully open. Her sensitivity was a fantastic asset. I relied on her.

Michael slept very little, about five hours with a few naps during the day. Pain prevented him from sleeping long periods--*no* position was comfortable.

"I can either scream or choke," he told me, describing the difference between sleeping propped up so that he could breathe or prone so that the pelvic tumor was less painful.

But in sickness or in health, Michael was so energetic that he required little sleep. He and Clairemarie talked late into the night and Michael often played his own compositions for her on his synthesizers. Michael did most of the talking. He liked to talk the way some people like to eat or shop or travel; that he could talk all night was a barometer of his strength. He was bouncing back.

And I was already exhausted and confused about how to take care of him. I comforted myself with the thought that I had brought Clairemarie to Michael and through his trust in me, he was better able to trust her. I had to make sure that he understood this triangle of trust, that he would accept Clairemarie in the role of his primary caregiver with me following her guidance, providing backup support like driving, laundry, groceries.

I told him how good Clairemarie was at taking care of people and that I wanted to make sure he felt all right about her as his primary caregiver.

"But you're my little sister."

"I know and I'll always be here for you, but she's nursed a lot of people who were sick. She took care of her dad when he had cancer and she's cared for people with malaria and other severe diseases in India."

"I know, but you're my little sister."

84

"I'll still be here to help, but she's a lot better at this o'kay? She told you that she'll stay. Please, let her be your caregiver."

"I want her to stay. It's o'kay."

Clairemarie applied a slippery elm poultice to Michael's back, later in the day, to help break up the copious mucous in his lungs.

"You'll never escape," he said. "I'm never letting you go back to California."

"Is that a promise?"

"No, it's a threat."

I fit into my caregiving role without anymore conflict until I found out, on July 5, that trimming Michael's toenails was not for the squeamish.

"These sure are nice slippers, Michael," I gagged as I pulled them off his feet.

"Aren't they wonderful?" He wiggled his toes. "Can you believe, I got them at Fred Meyer."

"Oh...I thought they were from Nordstrom."

"Nope. *Freddies.*"

"After I trim your nails, would you like your slippers cleaned? Your feet would probably feel really good."

"I guess," he said absently as I washed and massaged his feet.

When I finished, I went to wash my hands and found Clairemarie.

"His slippers are going to kill all of us."

"I'll clean them. No problem," she volunteered.

Michael constantly asked Clairemarie, in such an innocent way, "Are my slippers ready?"

After he asked yet again, in the late afternoon, I went with Clairemarie to the kitchen to check on the beloved slippers.

"Oh, no," I groaned. "Clairemarie, didn't you know these are leather?"

"*Leather?*" she screamed. "I thought they were synthetic! Why didn't you tell me?"

"Because you only had them in the sun. I didn't know you would put them in the oven and bake them to a crisp."

"No, I soaked them in a bucket of water with baking soda, too!"

She held up a baked slipper on the half-sole.

"Oh, my god. I *have* to get him a new pair. Don't tell him," she pleaded. "I don't want him to know these are ruined. *He loves them so much.*" She was in tears.

"He got those at Fred Meyer."

"Who's Fred Meyer?"

"He's a department store. Like Kmart."

"Take me there *right now.*" Still holding the toasted slipper, she charged for her purse and out the door before I reached for the car keys.

Already half crazed, Clairemarie went mad at the slipper display, rifling through every pair. But to no avail. Michael's slippers were nowhere to be found. She pounded the racks. A clerk, roused by the noise, appeared in the department.

"You got something that looks like this?" Clairemarie slammed a slipper on the counter.

"Oh, I think we've got one of that style left." She strolled off to the stock room, glancing back at us.

The clerk returned with an identical pair that by an act of God were Michael's size.

"*I'll take it.*" Clairemarie threw twenty-five dollars, a quarter of her life savings, at the clerk, hugged the slippers to her chest, and fled to the car.

"Fred Meyer, my savior! I got the last pair!" she yelled down the aisles.

"He's going to need these soon," she panted in the car. "He knows they should be dry by now."

"You really think it's such a big deal?"

"Drive!"

"Yes, sir."

We got back to the house and Clairemarie grabbed a pad of steel wool to scuff the soles. Then she gave Michael his slippers.

"Ooo," he cooed, "how'd you get them so clean? They look like new."

Clairemarie didn't want to ruin anything for Michael, not even his slippers. Michael waited until the quiet hours of the night and softly said to her, "I know."

But, his knowledge of her respect and love for him was tested when Beth talked on the phone one night with Clairemarie.

"So, have you jumped him yet?" Beth teased.

"No, not yet."

Michael's acute hearing picked up the question while Clairemarie held the phone down the hall from his room.

"Yeah, well," he said dejectedly from his bed, "who would want a limp rag like me anyway?"

Clairemarie gave me the phone and went to Michael.

"Do you think I wouldn't love you because of your body? Because you have cancer? Because you're bald and your leg is in a brace? Because you have a catheter in your chest? I love you. The cancer is beside the point."

"Well, you should have seen me before."

She told him again how much she loved him, *him*, and countered every physical aspect with how beautiful he was, what a noble heart he had and what a grand spirit he was. She reminded him that she had not come just to take care of his body, but all of him because she simply loved him. Cancer was beside the point.

Soon a crisis cemented Michael's trust in Clairemarie, in her motives for being with him, as a four day series of severe sciatic attacks began abruptly on July 6.

His pelvic tumor pressed into the nerve, burning him with pain of acute onset. The first attack happened while Michael waited in his room for Clairemarie and me to make lunch. Fifteen minutes had gone by when we both wondered why he had not come downstairs yet. I went to his room and found him standing, doubled over the bed, crying in agony.

"It's as bad as twelve years ago!"

"O'kay, Michael," I kept my voice level, calm. "We'll help you get through this." I ran to the hall.

"Clairemarie, get up here *now.*" *Get up here.*" I ran back to Michael.

"When did this start?"

"Just now...you were already coming up the stairs. Your timing is right as usual." He clawed the bed.

Only an hour had gone by since his last dose of painkillers--percoset. He would not take another dose because he did not want to become victim to the narcotic cycle of taking more and doing less. In general, his ability to hold out until the last moment created pandemonium when that last moment hit. But right now, the painkillers were not even working. I was ready to call the hospital for an ambulance and morphine, but Clairemarie was closer and, I felt, better.

With a combination of learned skill and instinct, she first eased Michael into bed, then asked him about the specifics of the pain. He kept a crushing grip on my hand as he relayed how the pain travelled down his leg. Clairemarie had no panic in her approach to Michael, now in screaming agony, only direct communication and action. The two of them quickly hit on a solution.

"Let's cut it off at the pass...put out the fire," Michael shook a fist at his leg.

"Heidi, we need cold water." Clairemarie sent me to the bathroom with a bucket and washcloths.

Michael pulled his pajama bottoms down from his hip and up from his calf and then Clairemarie did the really hard part. At his cue, she placed the cold cloths on Michael's hip, calf, and ankle with a slow but steady movement. The initial shock of the cold brought him to a higher level of pain. He pounded his fists into the bed, screaming into his pillow. The cold cloths started to block the pain within two minutes. The edge of relief came over us.

We kept applying the cold cloths for another fifteen minutes. The heat from the cloths burned my hand when I rinsed them in the bucket. I could only imagine what that heat felt like in Michael's ravaged body.

The pain stopped, leaving Michael exhausted and collapsed, but also hungry. Clairemarie and I hurried to the kitchen to finish making lunch. Michael's hunger could only weaken him more. Clairemarie returned upstairs with a plate of crackers and a thrown together tofu-cucumber salad (I threw the tofu and cucumber to her from the refrigerator). She knelt by Michael's bed.

With a shaking hand, he lifted the fork and tried to eat.

"Michael, let me do this," Clairemarie took the fork from his hand.

She fed him a bite size piece of cracker with the tofu salad. He loved it.

"Cheep cheep cheep," he sang when he wanted another bite.

Clairemarie fed him another cracker. He not only sounded like a baby bird, he looked like one, too, nested in his pillows, a fuzzy down on his otherwise bald head.

"Cheep cheep cheep."

Another cracker.

So it went until he finished his cheep cheep cheep lunch.

For Clairemarie, Michael's adorable bird song was a crucial turning point. She felt the permanence of his trust in her.

Michael slept after lunch while Clairemarie and I cleaned the kitchen. I took this time to beat myself up for not knowing how to fully handle Michael in overwhelming pain. I never realized until I was faced with caring for a very ill person, who also happened to be my brother, how natural it was for me to nurse animals and how hard it was to nurse humans. It was more than training, more than skill. I have an affinity for taking care of animals. I stood in the kitchen berating myself for what I saw as my deficiency in caring for humans.

Clairemarie kindly came right back at me, pointing out that people who take care of humans often do not do as well caring for animals. Clairemarie could handle anything with Michael, however urgent, however painful, however flipped out he was--or I was--but to see an animal in pain brings her to her knees. At least, she argued, I had the advantage of some caregiving experience, surely unlike so many thousands of other families and friends.

I felt better, too, when I verified what she said. I took a simple, informal survey, throughout the summer, of doctors and nurses in human and animal medicine. One nurse enjoyed human brain surgery and delightedly described how the skull is sawed open. But when I mentioned vaccinating her cat, she turned white and almost passed out. My "survey" helped me to see ability not deficiency.

Ability. In the time that Clairemarie cared for Michael, she met every demand, sometimes out of skill, sometimes by the seat of her pants, always out of love for him. She slept only two to three hours every single night and the only reason she has ever found for what sustained her indomitable care is that she loved Michael so much that she just did not want to miss anything. While so many people around us expected her to burn out if not drop dead, Clairemarie--even to her own amazement--never flagged. The meaning of grace to me was her care of my brother. This friend of mine, Clairemarie.

I have a deep respect for people who care for someone with a critical illness because to do so is an avalanche of stress in every sense. This respect arises out of Clairemarie's care of Michael and it is a respect that I have come to have for myself. While I can never know how I will respond in an extreme situation until I am in it, I always hope that I will be able to live with the consequences of my actions if I ever go through extreme adversity--like a war, like a killer disease. I do not know who I might become in the circumstances of a war, or if my own body were terribly ill, but I do know that when Michael suffered, I stood up to life and I stood up to death. With Michael and Clairemarie, I tapped into the mystery of our resourcefulness as human beings to care, endure, and prevail.

As cancer threw me full force into the maelstrom of the ill and dying, I found out what I was made of amidst all the pain, all the fear, and all of the confusion. I found out that I was brave, but bravery when I met it was not like I had imagined it to be. I was brave because I was afraid, but went ahead anyway. And I learned as I went along. The alternative was no alternative at all.

Every time that I thought I would lose it--which was often--I remembered what my Uncle Dan told me after he cared for Sadie, his mother, my grandmother, who died of heart disease only a few months before Michael's recurrence.

"I had to look at myself in the mirror--the next day."

I wanted to do that, too, if ever a tomorrow would be.

We had to get Michael ready to undergo another round of chemotherapy.

"Every time I need more rest, the cancer has more time to kill me," he told Dr. Frank, his oncology resident at their appointment, July 7.

Michael was warned--and not for the first time--that the chemotherapy could kill him as well. He insisted that he would be able to handle the treatment.

"Clairemarie and Heidi are here to help me, too. I feel much stronger since they got here."

Michael remained, as usual, intent and optimistic, ready to do something to fight the cancer even if that something might kill him.

The debilitating effects of pneumothorax on top of the cancer and chemo lengthened the interval between chemo sessions from three weeks to four. A week is a long time for osteogenic osteosarcoma. If his blood counts and strength stabilized by Monday, July 13, then he would go to St. Vincent for the next and possibly last round of chemotherapy. Everything that orthodox American medicine could offer short of an experimental program was riding on this next round. It had to do significant damage to the cancer, not just slowing the metastatic rate but stopping it and shrinking the tumors. A CAT scan would be run July 28 to determine this. If this arsenal of drugs did not work then we would have to find an experimental program, or go to Munich if Klinikum rechts der Isar had something to offer, or take the route of alternative therapies.

We also took our good news where we could get it. Dr. Frank was surprised that Michael did not have a much worse time with sciatica throughout his illness because of how closely situated the pelvic tumor was to the nerve. In that context, Michael felt lucky.

Back home, Michael wanted to write with me. He sat me down at the Mac, generously loaned to him by his friends, Victor and Sue, in an effort to help conserve his strength while he wrote. Michael stood next to me, teaching me how to use the word processor. In the middle of talking about nouns and verbs, Michael started to cry.

"I'm so glad you're here!" He was sobbing now.

He completely choked me up. We held each other, crying for a long time.

"I always told you I'd be here."

"I'm so glad."

The times when Michael cried with that raw pain, expressing his gratitude for my being with him, were the most poignant moments in my life, when the only thing that mattered was simply to love him.

Crying with Michael in front of the computer was a scene repeated throughout the summer not just with myself but with other loved ones as well.

He came up to Clairemarie one day and insisted she come to the computer. He wanted to show her *Harper*, the only writing of his that he insisted she see. I came out of the kitchen to see Michael sitting before the computer while Clairemarie read over his shoulder. By the end of the piece, she was crying beyond control.

"Isn't his writing incredible?" I said.

"No, it's *him*," she wept, her arms around Michael who sat crying with her.

"You won't be alone if you die," she said. "I promise, you won't be alone."

The practicalities of actually getting a harp to Michael's house were up in the air. Clairemarie made arrangements to take an extended leave of absence from her job, possibly losing her job altogether, except for one week in mid-July when she would return for five days to work and collect her belongings--like her harp. Or so we thought until she talked to Marni, the Portland distributor from whom Clairemarie had bought her harp.

Clairemarie had called Marni to discuss how to ship the harp to Portland. While playing phone tag, Marni, who knew nothing of Michael, got the very outgoing message he had recorded on his answering machine.

Michael yells as Phantom of the Opera type organ music plays:

95

"No, I'm out of apples! The doctor's have got me...*aaahh*!!"

Then, in his creepiest Igor voice:

"We have Michael at St. Vincent Hospital. If you're lucky you can reach him through patient info. Two, nine, one, two, one, one, five. Heh, heh, heh."

Marni left a wary message asking Clairemarie--if she really was at this number--to call back in the evening.

Her suggestion to Clairemarie was to loan her a shipping case for the harp or to rent a harp to her in Portland. Marni was less than thrilled with the idea of Clairemarie's harp being shipped. She related to this instrument like kin and wanted to take no risks with a long distance move. She invited Clairemarie to her home to talk about it and see what other harps were available, but their visit would have to wait until Michael was in the hospital and Clairemarie felt that she could afford some time away from him.

All efforts continued toward preparing Michael for chemotherapy. Clairemarie revolutionized his diet, changing almost everything except the plain acidophilus yogurt that he ate daily. She put him on a fat free diet, except for flax seed oil, and simple, bland organic foods rich with vegetables. She hooked up her water purifier and her water distiller, plugged in her Champion Juicer, and sorted her herbs. Because of his friend, Leesa, who was in medical school, he already was taking high doses of antioxidant vitamins, A, C, and E. And, then, in the midst of all of Clairemarie's hard work came the biggest source of conflict with Michael: butter. He loved buttery, spicy foods and chocolate and then she came along armed with a stack of books on cancer and nutrition and a will as strong as his.

"I want a pad of butter," he said into his bowl of hot cereal.

"Butter isn't good for you, Michael."

"I hate flax seed oil. I want a pad of butter," he held up a spoonful of cereal and watched it plop back into the bowl.

"Michael, I know this is really hard, but butter really is not good for you."

"*I want a pad of butter!*" he screamed.

And he got it.

"I will not, not *ever*, give up chocolate."

Clairemarie met the chocolate condition, but the butter fights broke out frequently.

Michael went into the hospital as scheduled on July 13. The night before, I walked down the hall toward my bedroom. He saw me from his bed and sweetly called my name.

"I'll be there in a sec, I have to put my dirty laundry down."

"I love you."

I dropped my bundle of laundry in the hall and went to him.

"I love you, too. You're the best brother in the world."

"I have a good role model."

We sat together in silence, smiling at each other.

Clairemarie spent the entire four days of hospitalization with Michael. The companionship was as vital as the constant physical attention. Although he was not coughing up as much mucous now as at the beginning of the month, which pleased him and his lung specialist, the chemo made him sweat profusely. Clairemarie kept a stack of sheets, towels, and hospital gowns in the room to keep pace with Michael as he soaked clothes and bedding non-stop. The nurses showed her the laundry supply room and encouraged her to help herself. Caregiving was, at least, as strenuous in the hospital as at home. She slept in a recliner if she slept at all, tending to Michael through the night.

I arrived at the hospital each morning to find her washing in a restroom in the ward.

"Don't you want more of a break?"

"Nope."

"Why not use the bathroom in Michael's room?"

"I don't want to disturb him."

I sometimes got her to go to the cafeteria with me if I played the Steinway that sat in the eating area. I can only play one song without music, *Song for Frances*, which I wrote for one of my cats who had passed away. Clairemarie never tired of hearing it. No one else in the cafeteria seemed to mind either. Michael, with his high musical standards, had given me the compliment, "That's not a bad piece of music."

In the evenings, Michael told Clairemarie that he had to exercise. He put on his robe and slippers, gripped his IV stand and, like a bull about to charge, put his head down and pushed his way around the oncology ward, stopping in patients' rooms to offer encouragement.

Clairemarie did spend one evening away from him, in a wonderland of harps, enchanted. Marni's storeroom, a huge living room in an elegant

98

old house, was packed with harps of all descriptions. Clairemarie looked like she had just entered heaven and music filled her night.

Marni listened compassionately as we told her about Michael and his harper. She offered Clairemarie a free loaner pedal harp, volunteering to deliver it. She also strongly discouraged Clairemarie from bringing her harp from the Bay Area, especially our idea to haul the harp 650 miles in my Toyota truck. We spent hours talking about what to do, considering everything, deciding nothing.

Only reluctantly did Clairemarie leave. She and I jockeyed potential harps for the rest of Michael's hospitalization, arguing against her harp because it was so much effort for possibly so little time. Borrowing a harp from Marni was more practical, we said. It would save time and money. It would be safer. Easier. Then, Clairemarie nailed us in a dangerous game.

"I'm bringing my harp."

"You are? Are you sure?"

"Yes. Don't you think it's really morbid and selfish of us to deny Michael my harp?"

"You mean, like he might go to Munich or die soon so why bother?"

"Yeah. Don't you find that really unfair?"

"Yes," I said guiltily. "I'm acting like he's an inconvenience."

"What difference does it make to us if we bring the harp for three months or three days? Michael will love it all the same."

"Then let's bring it. Otherwise, it's like we're waiting for him to die which is definitely not why we're here."

Michael left St. Vincent on Thursday, July 16 with a portable oxygen tank in case of any respiratory distress. A stationary unit, an oxygen convertor, was to be delivered at home later in the day.

Again our plans had changed for Michael's care. Not only was Clairemarie going back to the Bay Area for a week, but I was going with her. Our financial state was so bad that I felt my strongest contribution would be to work full time, to contribute money. With Beth's continued help, I figured that we could support Michael and Clairemarie with our paychecks until the government finally provided Social Security for him and state caregiver money for both Clairemarie and myself. If and when that government assistance happened, we would be able to survive financially and all be together. Michael supported my idea to go back to California for one to two week stretches to earn money and then return to Portland for visits. I would be commuting, but it seemed to work for us financially.

Michael, Clairemarie, and I had many people to thank for helping us survive: my employers for being so flexible; Beth for giving us her savings and running her credit cards up to the limit only to regret that she did not have more to give; Jiya, for subletting Clairemarie's apartment, paying her bills, and taking care of Mu the Cat; Michael's and my sister, Cheryl, with her own family in San Diego, for helping with the rent.

100

We arranged through the State of Oregon to have a caregiver help Michael while we were gone. We felt relatively secure about Michael being without us for five full days and he did his best to assure us that he would be all right.

"If I'm not, I'll call you."

"Promise," we both said.

"I'll call you."

We would leave for the Bay Area on Friday, July 17 and return to Portland the following Friday. Clairemarie would finish her business, I would earn survival money, and then we would pack the harp in my truck and go home to Michael. I was to keep my promise and deliver a harp and a harper to play for him.

Just as Sisters of Providence came along not a moment too soon to provide health care for Michael, Clairemarie came along not a moment too soon to care for him. Michael always seemed to live his life in the nick of time. Suspense never eluded him or anyone who loved him. Living with Michael was like being struck by lightning. Twice.

Chapter 12 The Taste of Hell

June 12, 1992

Oh dear God, not again. That awful sweet metallic taste, the unmistakable flavor of Cisplatin. It's back and I can't tell if my growing nausea is not also some trigger response held over from twelve years ago, co-joining with this new poisoning to see if I can't have just a little bit more misery. Yet, just shortly ago, hours after being released from St. Vincent, I felt fine. It was a rough go of it, with the Bleomycin knocking me for a loop and the urgent need of a thoracentesis to drain 2060 cc of fluid from my right lung before I choked to death. Still, it went well, as cancer treatments go. Until now.

Perhaps I have had it too easy, felt too good, done too well. Perhaps it is a necessary part of this often rotten process to get sicker than Hell and to have that Hell linger on your pallet like a putrid wine whose vintage is worse than abysmal.

And the god-damn ringing in my ears is back, also with a vengeance. I cannot turn it off and it will not go away. It will drive me nuts, but only if I let it. Not an easy task, considering I won't be getting any reprieves to catch my breath, or anything else for that matter.

I remember telling Dr. Mastanduno last Friday, just before I was to undergo this latest cycle of chemotherapy, a changed one because the first regimen hadn't reduced the cancer, that I hadn't survived twelve years ago by playing it safe, let alone comfortable, and that the same was even more true this time, given my cancer is metastatic.

"Push it to the wall, through the wall," I had told him. We did. And now I feel like shit with the Taste of Hell in my mouth and nothing in the world capable of washing it away.

Please, don't think I am complaining. I'm not. It is just a tired, war-weary observation that the battle is getting a bit more ferocious. And so shall I be. But I will find a way of being peacefully ferocious, even in the midst of being nastily sick, because I made a choice to find another way besides anger, besides resentment, besides hatred. I have too much love in my life to ever, ever choose that path again. So now I must wander down this most arduous road with only Love as a guide, my friends and family as companions, and the Taste of Hell to spur me on. I think they will be more than enough. In fact, I swear to Love they will be.

Chapter 13 Sex and the Cancer Patient

June 11, 1992

Yes.

Chapter 14 Sex and the Cancer Support Person

Whenever.

Chapter 15 Lay Down Comedy

We make use of our physical senses in one way or another throughout our lives, usually without thinking twice about it if ever at all. But when our bodies fail us, as Michael's failed him, there is still a higher sense, what I would call a human sense: the sense of humor. This only rarely failed Michael and then only in the very worst of times, transiently. Michael stayed humorous overall as his body pained him relentlessly, as he became increasingly ill and bedridden, and as he lay dying.

Even when he did lose his sense of humor, his ill temper was of late onset, the last couple weeks of his life, and was never as bad as it could have been, especially given how massively ill he had been for months. Often he seemed so vital that people did not believe he had advanced stage cancer or even the flu. Still, much to my horror, I found that a long inactivated and not so extinct button was being pushed; namely, I'm-afraid-of-my-big-brother. Michael was a Grouch and it took me a good week to realize that it was not personal. He did it to everyone.

Michael needed to have his body massaged almost constantly for pain relief. He often said, "...rubs, more rubs... ." One night, he asked

106

Clairemarie to massage his back. While she worked his muscles, he told her to shift up and to the right. When she missed the exact point, he barked and jabbed his thumb in the four directions, "No! That's up! That's down! That's right! That's left!"

Clairemarie has travelled all over the world, so Michael's back was not exactly uncharted territory, requiring a compass. Besides that, he *had* drawn a map of his body for her when she first came to care for him.

She said, "Michael, I need a map of your body, so I won't cause you any discomfort."

He took an illustrative approach to this request, an illustration of which, that compass night, he should have been reminded. Michael sketched a lesson in anatomy, a stick figure with a squared-off head and diagrammatically labeled: *zee head part, eez okay to touch wiss zee various bodily partz!; zee neck part (good for zee wringing!); zee Groshong Catheter, NOT good to touche; zee place where zee poke in zee beeg chest holes; zee lint collector, play at your own risque; zee feetsies, good for zee massage, but tickling eez zee beeg death; on zee back--zee deadly pain in the ass. Keep off! MOTHER!!; zee most beeg, new and very German knee, do not touch except eef you are suicidal.* And with an arrow to the crotch, *touch by Rx only.*

So, Michael fell off his own mappe, see *zee neck part.* He lapsed into being a grouch, a leveler of scathing comments and looks. I had not seen him like this since B.C., before cancer, before 1980.

Throughout his teenage years, he had seethed about life, masking and protecting his emotional wounds. Michael, hermetically sealed with rage, kept everyone away. No one could get anywhere near him to hurt

107

him. No one could get anywhere near him to love him either and that pained me the most. Twelve years of my breaking through his barriers, which many people could never do, seemed in jeopardy to me. That is what I feared now and that is what I had to transcend.

It took one enema--given to Michael not me.

Days went by, in July, after the last round of chemotherapy, before Michael was convinced that an enema would help him. He, like most, in response to the "E" word cringed and balked, but Clairemarie persisted, knowing that an enema would be a simple way to help detoxify his body. His doctors even said it would be an o'kay thing to do. I was a little surprised at the level of his resistance; after all, here was a man who unflinchingly braved multiple, major orthopedic surgeries, involving the internal amputation of part of his right femur, part of his tibia, and his whole knee except the patella, having all of it replaced with a prosthesis. Here was a man who worked so painstakingly hard to regain all the mobility that he possibly could and then some, and then went on with his life as an athlete and coach of fencing. Without a limp. Here was a man who braved umpteen rounds of aggressive chemotherapy. But an enema? *An enema?* In the privacy of his own home? We may as well have offered to pull all of this teeth. Michael's intestinal motility was ruined by one of the common, miserable effects of the chemotherapy that he underwent. He finally acquiesced to an enema when he realized that he was just plain constipated. As if having a huge hemorrhoid from straining after his first round of chemo, in April, was not enough to prove it.

After this one enema, I understood that his crabby behavior was a measure of ill health and not ill will. He felt so much better after one cleansing that he kept asking for more in order to flush his overloaded body of the toxins from chemo and cancer. While Michael received his enemas, he would speak in his most pious voice, acting like a holy man. These outward displays of irreverence for internal bodily purification forever banished all of our enema jokes, hemorrhoid included, to the realm of bend over comedy.

"The way to enlightenment is through the life giving waters that descend from the Great Bag Above, cleansing the impure lower centers..."

He carried on with this monologue while Clairemarie tried to maintain the position of the tube and the flow and pressure of the water. Invariably, she would laugh really hard while Michael jabbered and the tube would slip. Great panic ensued as the tube impaled Michael's poor hemorrhoid and he would yell out in a resounding, mundane voice. For everyone involved, fortunately, Clairemarie could make a quick recovery, so all was not lost.

"The cleansed path to enlightenment..." he would sigh in a state of equanimous grace, surrendering to the inevitable.

Later on, once Michael was back in bed, he would call to me, make a victory sign, and boast, "I took *two* bags full." He was so proud of himself.

"Gee, that's really good," I'd say. "I doubt I could do that much!" I was proud of him, too, because he always found a way to positively engage himself in his healing no matter how taboo or gross something was to our minds.

By the end of July, Michael could barely move away from his bed, so trips to the bathroom for more cleansings were not possible, but because enemas gave him so much relief, he kept asking Clairemarie, "Do we have time for an enema?"

Thanks to St. Vincent's Home Care delivery services, we coped with the logistical problems of Michael's privy, but we had to wait all day. Finally, at 7 p.m., Michael's adaptive equipment (a.k.a. the port-o-potty) arrived. In true Jungian fashion, a phenomenal synchronicity took place. Just as the adaptive equipment crossed the threshold of the house, a Catholic priest, sent by one of our Jewish relatives, walked up to the door.

I was stunned by the coincidence. The delivery man was embarrassed. The priest smiled graciously and went inside. I burst out laughing and praised the powers that be for bringing a little levity to a plastic chair that only represented to me just how bad things were getting.

The port-o-potty. Michael loved that thing. Clairemarie padded it with thick pieces of foam and it became the most comfortable furniture for sitting to come Michael's way since the pelvic tumor had started to hurt so many months ago. It actually was the only comfortable furniture for sitting that we found for him. Perhaps the idea could be developed for others with similar pelvic pain. I considered taking out a patent on padded port-o-potties for pelvic pain. Priest available separately by divine intervention.

So, as difficult as it had been for me initially to deal with Michael's bad moods, and the hermetic seal of unlovability that previously was at their core, I knew it was necessary to distinguish between the Former Scathing Grouch Self and the Present Scathing Toxic Ill Self. While the behavior appeared the same, the motivations were different. I stayed focused on the fact that I loved Michael and he knew it, and that he loved me and I knew it, too. The tapestry did not fray or unravel.

Once he felt less toxic and less miserable after that one legendary enema, Michael became genuinely polite again, too, instead of rude and impatient with a perfunctory *please* and *thank you*. Most of all, he became ornery and funny again.

No one was ever immune to Michael's humor; especially not doctors, not nurses and his home caregiver, not fellow patients, not the IRS, and definitely not little sisters. Michael's sense of humor remained intact, wildly so at times, often confined to bed as he was. He uplifted everyone around him if we were not too busy crawling out of the room, clutching our bellies, begging him to stop. Michael was a great jester regardless and sometimes because of how miserable circumstances were. He utilized his sense of humor to transform a very unfunny, life threatening condition into a playful mode of detachment and understanding. His antics made me aware, at least, that no one is and no one needs to be merely the condition of his or her body.

Michael proved beyond all doubt that an apple a day will keep the doctor away.

One day, Michael saved his apple from lunch and kept it on the cart near his hospital bed. He figured he would eat it later with his antibiotics until something or rather, someone, better came along.

When his oncologist, Dr. Mastanduno, showed up with his stethoscope poised to listen to Michael's chest, Michael snatched the apple and held it up to the good doctor's face, yelling, "Get back, you Son of the AMA!"

Then Michael hauled himself out of bed, his typically oversized hospital gown trailing behind him, and hobbled after Dr. Mastanduno, all the while waving the apple like a lunatic. He chased his doctor out into the hall and triumphantly brandished the apple for all to see. Standing there bald, in a huge nightgown with his IV stand clutched in one hand and his magic apple clutched in the other, he was a formidable sight.

Dr. Mastanduno, talking like Dracula, shot back over his shoulder, "It'll take a lot more than one of those to cure what you've got!"

Teasing doctors paled in comparison to the type of women with whom Michael spent way too much time. Here is a retrospective sampling of that cherished group, the female nurses.

Michael was hospitalized at St. Vincent for another round of chemotherapy. Although sedated in the evenings while the chemo was administered, he would wake up if someone entered his room because not even sedation could blunt how acutely aware of his surroundings he always was.

112

One night, a nurse came in and, seeing him awake, asked, "Have you seen the IV nurse?"

Drowsily, he lifted up his blankets, looked underneath, and said, "She's not in here." Then he fell back to sleep.

The next afternoon, when he really was awake, the entire nursing crew reminded him of how he had helped fine the IV nurse.

In keeping with his reputation at St. Vincent, fully established after he wrote the shortest chapter in the history of literature and medicine, *Sex and the Cancer Patient*, his nurses wrote out a discharge instructions form and marked the box for sex, then wrote in, *prn*, as needed. Michael loved showing his prescription to everyone...er, the form from the hospital, that is.

But he really left his heart and at least, one pair of Jockey underwear, in Munich, at Klinikum rechts der Isar. Given the German style of communal rooms, Michael found a camaraderie with his fellow patients during the winter of 1980-'81 that he never forgot and, when hospitalized in America, always missed, especially the fun and games which invariably involved the nurses.

Making the Best of It

Not everything that happens in the course of long term hospitalization is to be despaired. After awhile, a hospital becomes a home, with the staff and fellow long term patients becoming something of an ersatz family. And, to relieve the tension born of the ofttimes grim nature of why we are all there, the members of this family joke and clown around.

To make a long story short, allow me to share some of the levity I perpetrated, ahem...*experienced*, during my stay in Klinikum rechts der Isar.

Burlesque

November 24, 1980

When you have a tumor, there is a grim elation when you are about to have that malignant, pain-giving life-eater cut out of you. I have seen this reaction often, and my own was no different. Up to the last moment, the pain had varied from hideously miserable to utterly intolerable, but it made little impression on my growing sense of impending freedom and victory in snatching my young life back from the Gates of Death.

I was overjoyed at passing up the evening meal the night before surgery, drawing nourishment instead from my burgeoning elation. I reached the ecstatic when the breakfast cart was wheeled into the room and all were fed, except me. The wretched, murderous lump was coming out and I was going to go on with my life, this just a brief terror along the way. By the time the nurses arrived with the "the needle", the pre-surgical injection that would send me on a grinning, trippy journey into lala-land, I was giddy with joy.

114

My roommates commenced the traditional pre-surgical chant: "Needle, needle, needle, needle...". Suddenly, a crazy, silly idea burst in my mind and to the rhythmic chant I began a slow, languorous strip tease. The two nurses stood stupefied, mouths agape as I peeled off my t-shirt, held it with two fingers of my sinuously undulating left hand, then let it float down to my bed, all the while giving them the wickedest of grins.

"Needle! Needle! Needle!" came the intensified chant as I slid my hands down my flanks, slipping fingers under the elastic band of my Jockey briefs.

"NEEDLE! NEEDLE! NEEDLE!" My roommates cried as I slowly worked my briefs past my hips, down my legs, and stepped out of them. With a flourish, I whipped my briefs over my head and began twirling them on my left index finger while I slowly gyrated into the center of the room. Abruptly, I shot my shorts across the room and they plopped onto Rudi's chest. Even though cancer had long ago put Rudi's nerves to the torch, he too joined in the pounding, wild scream, "NEE-DLE! NEE-DLE! NEE-DLE!"

The nurses' eyes were bulging as I wiggled and squirmed over to the table by the window. Once there, I thrust out my rump, patting it, inviting one of them to do her duty and jab me with the needle. Suddenly, I shot bolt upright as someone slapped me hard on my rear-end and a brief, burning sensation followed a quick jab of the needle. I turned to find myself staring up into the chief surgeon's annoyed face.

My roommates were howling and laughing hysterically, sometimes hacking and choking.

"Well, ladies," the chief surgeon inquired testily, "haven't you ever seen a naked man before?"

"But, Herr Professor, he was, well..." Poor Eva just couldn't seem to find a way to describe what had just transpired. She did, however, manage to catch me up and lay me on the gurney, just as I began to giggle and blubber nonsense; the shot worked fast. Ulrike, the other nurse, covered me up while the surgeon departed for the scrub room, shaking his head.

About the last thing I cogently remember was wild applause and Uma whispering in my ear, "We'll get you for this."

Ulrike and Eva never did get me back for my little burlesque, but to this day I do not know what ever became of my dark blue Jockey shorts.

Close Shave

November 1980

Before the orthopedic surgeons could remove the tumor from behind my right knee, they needed to know the precise locations of the blood vessels in that area. Therefore, I was to undergo an angiogram; that is where the doctors insert a catheter to inject the target area with special dye and then take x-rays. Two days before the angiogram I was given a waiver to sign. It stated that this procedure was safer than

116

driving from Munich to Nuremburg. Given the way West Germans drive, that was small comfort. But, the procedure being critical, I signed the waiver and found myself being prepped two days later by Rosemarie, the head nurse.

Rosemarie was a stern, distant woman. There was absolutely no doubt as to her professional competence, but most of us would rather have hugged a block of ice. I was not thrilled to see her advancing upon me, razor in hand.

"Michael, it is time to prepare you for your angiogram. Please, accompany me to the bathing room."

Our ward consisted of four communal patient rooms, with a separated WC and bathing facilities, examining room, nurses' station, doctors' room, and the operating room at the far end of the corridor.

I looked at Rosemarie, swallowed hard, gathered up my crutches, and hobbled after her to the sounds of my roommates humming a well known German dirge. When I arrived in the bathing area, there sat Rosemarie on a low, folding stepstool, the razor in hand. With full professional detachment, I was ordered to drop my pants.

"My girlfriend will be jealous," I offered lamely, trying to prevent the inevitable.

"I can hardly see why," came Rosemarie's professionally innocent reply.

"Thanks a lot!" I growled indignantly.

Then I saw the unbelievable: Rosemarie trying to hide a blush. It would have been the time to push the joke a bit farther if not for her splashing veeeeery cooooold waaaaater on my crotch, grabbing my privacy, and starting to shave the appropriate area. Even less funny was that this method was basically pulling out the hair, not shaving it.

With a yelp of pain and indignation, or was that pained indignation?, I knocked the razor out of Rosemarie's hand, hiked up my pajama bottoms, and hurried back to my room, setting a new world record in the 20 meter hobble.

"Michael! Get back here! I have not yet finished shaving you!"

"The hell you haven't, Rosemarie!" I screamed. "I'll do it myself! I happen to plan on using this thing some time in the future!"

Most of the ward, including several elderly ladies, were laughing heartily. I would have been laughing, too, if not for the fact that those were my private parts at serious risk. I got back to the wash area of my room, broke out my shaving cream and razor, and set myself to the task of saving my yet unborn future generations, before Rosemarie could get to me with her razor. When she arrived a few moments later, the area in question was covered in shaving cream and I was dutifully prepping myself.

Her only comment was a brusk, "I will stay to ensure that you have done it properly."

Once I was prepped and in radiology, the intern chirped, "Oh my, what a lovely prep job! I have never seen a patient so smoothly shaved. Which nurse did this?"

"I did it myself."

"Really? You didn't want a nurse to shave you?"

118

I could only sigh and wonder why Rosemarie and her razor had not been stated in the waiver as one of the major risks of an angiogram.

What's My Size

March 1981

I would like to know who is in charge of hospital laundry services. I have been in lots and lots of hospitals and the story seems to be a universal one: they never have your size cleaned when you need it most. In German sizing, I take a 46, which is so uncommonly small that they haven't had much use for it with adults since the Middle Ages when I would have been on the tallish side (sigh...). Well, courtesy of my reactions to strong doses of chemotherapy, I had made quite a mess of myself, so it was time for a change of bed clothes--my second of the day. Of course, there were no size 46's to be had in the entire hospital, which is one of the largest in former West Germany. My nurse, a young Bavarian who was smaller than I am, brought me the only other set of bed clothes available--size 56. David and Goliath could have shared these pajamas. My protests went unheeded, in large part because we lacked an alternative.

Picture a five foot-three inch tall, cue-ball friseured fellow hooked up to an IV, standing there on one leg (my knee replacement was too recent to put weight on my right leg) in his grossly over-sized light blue hospital pajamas. The sleeves were over eighteen inches too long, the bottom hem of the top hanging past my knees. In fact, I could have fit myself into the top sideways. And, of course, there were the pants...I was holding them up with my left hand, which was also holding the crutch, while my IV slowly dripped into my right forearm.

(The remainder of the story has snickering and giggling for background music...)

"Baerbel, dear, these pajamas are really too large."

"Nonsense. Besides, Michael, that's the only one we've got. You'll have to live with it until the laundry..."

"Nonsense to you, too! There is no laundry. It is a plot by this hospital to make me wear pajamas that you could park a BMW in."

"It's not that bad...is it?" Bingo.

"Oh, yeah? Well, here." I let go of my trousers, which promptly curled themselves around my ankles. At this, Baerbel--and my four roommates--burst into laughter. Baerbel clung in vain to the wall, slowly sinking to the floor like a sunset, her face glowing red.

Full Pants

March 1981

One of my fellow patients was suffering from a gruesome blood illness, the treatments for which left him hopelessly incontinent. For proprietous Germans, this has to rank as a most vile fate, constantly soiling your britches in a room full of other patients. Otto, needless to say, was often extremely depressed and we always tried to cheer him up. One day, fate played right into our hands.

Father Bernhard, a Benedictine monk with as outrageous a sense of humor as any mortal being I have met, received a bar of chocolate from one of his acolytes who had just returned from a trip to Switzerland. The young brother set the bar on the nice marble ledge below the window before he left and wished us all a speedy recovery. Well, we all had visitors and did not notice the chocolate bar slowly turning to chocolate sauce. You see, underneath the nice marble ledge was the nice, warm radiator.

"Oh, blessed saints," sighed Father Bernhard in his most pontifical style. "Alas, my lovely chocolate hath turned to soup. What shall we ever do with it now...?" I was actually startled at the quirky smile that was slowly spreading across the Benedictine's face, despite my knowing him for over a month. Then I caught on.

"You don't actually mean...? Yes! Let's do it!" I squealed with glee. Our other roommates chortled expectantly.

"Do what?" moaned Otto. "If you are trying to think of some gag, well, I just want to sleep."

"Spoil-sport!" I teased. "Besides, if I have correctly guessed the Reverend Father's intent, your assistance is critical."

"Indeed, my sons. For behold my plan..."

A few minutes later, Otto rang for the nurse.

"I'm sorry, Ruth," Otto pleaded. "God, I hate this. I've...oh, I'm so sorry." Otto was now on the verge of tears. What a performance!

Ruth was one of those gems you always hope to have as a nurse: sweet, compassionate, light-hearted, and highly competent.

"Hey, it's all right. I understand and don't think that this is dirty. You just lie there and I will clean you up." Ruth's voice was very soothing, in part because of her soft, lilting Franconian accent, but mostly because her words came from her heart.

We were all hiding our faces in our pillows while Ruth got a warm towel to clean up Otto's bottom. It was a good thing that the young lady was guileless or we would have been found out in a wink:

"Here we go. I'll have you all cleaned in just a...O mein Gott!"

Now we were howling with unrestrained laughter and within seconds, Ruth was laughing no less than we were, for there on Otto's bottom was a heart with " I love you, Nurse", drawn in one nicely melted chocolate bar.

Michael had lots of fun and games in 1992, especially with Clairemarie. He did so beginning with an ironclad grip on her.

He loved to grab her attention whenever he was in bed. Clairemarie would lean over to adjust his sheets and blankets and pillows and Michael would grab her blouse with his dexterous toes and hold on like a crab. When she tried to straighten up, she found herself held fast by Michael's toehold. After caring for Michael for only a few days, Clairemarie knew he would try to grab her blouse with his toes, but he simply used her sense of anticipation as a bigger challenge to grab her by surprise. The days when she wore a long skirt gave Michael an even greater advantage. Clairemarie would be halfway across the room, sure she was free of his hold on her, only to find herself stuck in mid-stride, her skirt yanked from behind.

Everyday became a tug of war between her shirt or skirt and his toes, so they did not exactly start off their relationship on the right foot but on Michael's foot.

For me, with my brother and my best friend in the same place at the same time, the potential for fun was irresistible.

One night, Clairemarie was cleaning up in the kitchen while Michael and I were in the adjacent dining room; he sitting, I standing next to him.

I noticed a bump on Michael's head, probably from getting whacked in Kendo or something and I became seized by the impulse of a practical joke.

"Michael," I said, projecting my voice enough for Clairemarie to overhear, "is that a scar from the electrode they put in your head?"

"Oh, yes," he replied, slightly raising his voice, too, "but it's not just a scar. The electrode is still in there."

"Wow! I thought they removed it years ago."

"Oh, no. They didn't. This is *it*!"

Clairemarie was trying really hard to mind her own business in the kitchen, but Michael and I smirked as we got our story rolling. We knew she heard us!

"That's really something," I said. "Since you are bald now, I can see it. I'd forgotten all about it. Hey, Clairemarie, did you know this?"

I was inviting her to take the bait. Michael and I were total dead pans.

"Know what?" She said, looking our way for the first time.

"C'mere. Did you know that Michael has an electrode in his head?" I was sounding rather scientific, I thought.

"He does?" She asked incredulously, standing in the doorway to the dining room, dish towel in hand.

"Oh, yes," said Michael. "See?" He pointed to his head.

"No, you don't," Clairemarie argued.

"Yes, I do. Would you like to touch it?" Michael bowed his head to her. "You know, I was an experimental case in 1980."

"Go ahead," I said, watching her step slowly toward him. She moved with caution, but her curiosity drew her inexorably closer. "Really, it's an electrode."

Michael nodded encouragingly.

Clairemarie extended a tentative index finger toward the bump on Michael's head. Slowly, slowly she came closer, while he and I remained stock still, poker faced.

And then, in one electrifying moment, she touched his head.

"Zzzst!" He yelled and jolted his body.

Clairemarie screamed and flew backwards a good three feet. Michael and I squealed with delight, burst into laughter, and shook hands. Three feet backwards meant that our practical joke scored in the

124

upper tenth percentile. But the fact that Clairemarie was laughing and screaming and we all started hugging each other made it one of the best of our jokes.

Clairemarie experienced the spectrum of Michael's humor, from the cute and charming to the downright fiendish.

Once, in the dead of night while hospitalized, Michael woke up in hysterics, screaming, "It's just like twelve years ago! It's just like twelve years ago!"

Clairemarie rang for the nurse immediately while Michael began to hyperventilate from fear, ripping at his clothes and IV lines.

"*It's just like twelve years ago!*"

Michael threw himself out of bed as the nurse rushed in.

"Get him to calm down!" She told Clairemarie and they both went to work.

"Michael, you have to calm down!" The nurse was direct and forceful. She got his attention.

Gently but firmly, Clairemarie kept repeating, "It's not twelve years ago, Michael. You're right here at St. Vincent. It's 1992. It's o'kay. You're here with me, Clairemarie. You're here with me."

Michael was still crying, but he started to relax and breathe regularly.

The nurse and Clairemarie changed him out of his sweat soaked clothing, dried him off, and changed his bedding.

"O'kay, Michael, let's get you back into bed now." The nurse helped him turn around, facing the bed.

With his back to them, Michael let out a murderous scream that must have shaken the entire ward. Clairemarie and the nurse crashed into each other, falling into the hospital equipment.

Michael slowly looked over his shoulder and said, "Heh, heh, heh."

He almost died that night once Clairemarie disentangled herself from the nurse.

Most of the time, however, I never knew what Michael did to Clairemarie. I only saw the result.

"Oh, there you are again," I often said upon entering Michael's room.

Clairemarie, under the bed, held her sides while Michael, in the bed, batted his eyes and repeated the magic word, "Truffles."

Some things are better left a mystery.

The IRS was not exempt from Michael. A few years before his recurrence, he owed money on his tax return. He endorsed his check to the IRS followed by a frowning smiley face with its tongue sticking out.

Then, in one of those bizarre coincidences when life is again stranger and certainly more painful than fiction, the day that Michael filed his 1991 tax return was the day he was diagnosed with a recurrence of cancer, April 9, 1992.

He quipped about the consummate joke, "Taxes are going to give me one thousand dollars back and death is giving me another run for it."

126

In honor of Michael, I encourage everyone who owes another dime to the government to draw a frowning smiley face with it tongue sticking out on all checks endorsed to the IRS.

As his Little Sister, I figured prominently in Michael's sense of humor, but of all the nutty things he ever did to me nothing rivaled the way he used his head to catch me off guard. Michael reflected on the evolution of...

My Life As A Streetlamp

May 5-12, 1992

"Does noon sound o'kay to you?" Leesa's voice is enthusiastic and cheerful as always.

"Ma'velous, da'ling, simply ma'velous. I shall be up, dressed, and have my head properly polished." If cheer and enthusiasm are infectious, then I am beyond treatment.

"Oh, no! My sunglasses can't block that much light!"

"Egads, I forgot. How about if I use dull-coat!"

"Wheew. That should do it. Pick you up at noon. See ya."

"Looking forward to it. Bye." What some folks will do for a trip up the Columbia River Gorge.

I run my hand over my scalp as I hang up the telephone, contemplating once again changing careers to, and this time I get really

127

creative, reflector on a guard rail along some scenic stretch of road. Twelve years ago, the last time I got a chemotherapy haircut and shave, seem like an eternity ago, but the zany humor about being shorter-haired than a shaved Chihuahua is still intact. Back then, I told individuals who found my chemotherapy-induced baldness disconcerting that I was applying for work as a streetlamp. After all, between a polished head and oodles of radiological exams, I should glow quite nicely in the dark. Other bad, evil, nasty, not nice puns almost ensured that I wouldn't survive cancer ("Nurse, hook up some curare to his IV--stat!")

Baldness is the most visible clue to the world that you are battling cancer. Toupees, hats, bandanas, paint, crepe paper, or, in my case, a latex Klingon forehead, it does not matter. Bald is bald. Facial hair falls out. Chest hair falls out. Pubic hair falls out (damn, and I had such a miserable adolescence, too). Worse, there are all these stinking Neo-Nazi Skinheads running loose: bald is just not politically correct and I cannot do a thing about it. *Pfui, Diefi*, as they say in Bavarian.

There are other problems, too. I keep slipping off my pillows and friends' shoulders. Worse, my head acts like either a solar cell or a refrigerator in accordance with the temperature. Maybe I'll keep the Klingon forehead on permanently and snarl a lot.

At least my hair is not a mess when I wake up and my friseur and shampoo bills are as nonexistent as my hair. Also, shaving is much safer: just try cutting yourself with soap, water, and a washcloth. There is a bright side to everything, especially when your head glows in the dark.

128

Of course, the setting is nine tenths of the battle. On May 4 and 6, I felt well enough to do a shift as a volunteer explainer at the Oregon Museum of Science and Industry where they have a great exhibit using *Star Trek* as a way of getting folks to explore real science. So, I donned my captain's uniform and hobbled out to spend a wonderful afternoon making science and learning fun.

Almost immediately, kids started asking me in hushed, awed tones, "Are you Captain Picard?"

The best I managed was, "No, he has more hair than I do--and he's taller, too." I pointed to Captain Picard on the laser disk and sighed. Hell, Sinead O'Connor has more hair than I do.

Being bald has some severe social drawbacks. A few days ago, I was in the bank and two African Americans looked at me with terror in their eyes, thinking I was a Skinhead. It was my sad duty to explain why I was bald and to assure them that I detest Skinheads utterly. Also, I have been heckled at by impudent wretches in passing cars, gawked at by passing louts, and frequently treated like a freak.

The same thing happened twelve years ago when I returned to the United States from Germany. No sooner had I debarked from the 1981 flight than the gawking and disgusted looks commenced. I am not paranoid, either. I started fighting back using humor and shock tactics, but I really wanted to be left alone instead of being treated like a freak released from some second-rate circus. I do not act like a victim, I do not curl up and totter about. I try to be just another bloke on the street.

I have gotten some flattering compliments and a few winks and nods.

Twelve years ago, I wore a wig. Wigs are wonderful. Wigs are useful. Wigs are great for making bad puns. Wigs also make great weapons. Nyahaha. But, I think I will let Heidi tell that part, especially since she bore the brunt of many of my wig pranks.

The year was 1981 and Michael was bald from chemotherapy, but he never flipped his wig. He tipped it. Imagine how starling it is to have someone pull his hair off as a gesture of greeting. Michael, the picture of a less than perfect gentleman, lifted his wig up, flashed his bald head and then set the wig back down, cocked over his eye. So suave, so cool, he sprang away on his crutches, leaving me dead in my tracks.

Wig tipping did become a welcome routine for me after the initial shock, but for the young children who knew Michael and did not understand why his hair was gone, he put them at ease right away.

"Would you like to pull my head off?" He asked his little friends.

"*Really?*" They were always wide-eyed.

"Yes, you may pull my head off. Here, pull on my hair with both of your hands."

"Neat!"

They took their small fists, grabbed his hair like he told them, and pulled back, often so forcefully as to plop on the ground, amazed at the sight of the wig in their hands.

"I pulled Michael's head off!" They would yell as if it were the greatest of discoveries.

The children had so much fun pulling his head off that they quickly found nothing strange about Michael being bald.

I was not so lucky. Just when I thought it was safe, always a mistake, Michael would pull something else on me.

Late one summer night in 1981, the house a quiet hush, Michael really made me flip over his wig with one premeditated prank.

Half asleep, I predictably made my way through the dark hallway to the bathroom adjacent to Michael's bedroom. I saw him reading in bed, seemingly oblivious to my presence. Continuing to the bathroom, I turned on the light, my eye catching one blinding sight of a furry dead thing on the counter.

I screamed and ran back into the hall, still squinting from the light. Then I saw Michael, chortling in bed, and I knew he had not been reading at all.

"Neep!" He roared.

"Neep," came my feeble reply. "Nice place to leave your wig for a change.

"Neep-ity neep!"

I was relieved when Michael wrote to me in the Spring of '92, "I know, I know, I'm warped, demented, and I wear a hat." Michael as a mad hatter was a relief. I could not bear to flip over his wig again.

Neep. In the beginning, as brother and sister, before there were wigs or electrodes or apples, there was The Word. The Alpha and the Omega of our Nonsense, spoken with deep affection and fun, meaning everything from *hello* to *I love you*, from *great* to *you really fell for that*. Or as Michael said, "To Neep or not to Neep. What a hell of a question."

Besides missing Michael *in toto*, what I clearly miss in particular is having fun with him. One of my greatest regrets was that he never met my little dog, Diggity. The two of them together would have made *Lay Down Comedy* roll over and play dead.

Well, enough of all this funny business. Remember Michael's warning: Anyone within earshot will be.

Neep.

Chapter 16 Journey to Elsewhere

"I know that I have to die, I'm just not ready to die right now," Michael's weak, lamenting voice came over the phone to Clairemarie in the Bay Area.

She and I were ready to leave for Portland the next morning, but our itinerary was changed by the urgency of Michael's call on Wednesday, July 22. We had been away five of our six days. Schedules always changed on this rollercoaster of disease. It required constant flexibility, everything prefaced with *if*. Michael was not doing well and we took the first available flight to Portland, Wednesday night.

Clairemarie had been the first to reach Michael by phone, in the afternoon, responding to a message left on both our answering machines to please come back to him as soon as possible. We had called him everyday, at least once, during our separation. He was holding his own, but it only took one bad day to dramatically change his stability. When I tried Michael and then Clairemarie only to find both lines busy, I waited. A cold sinking feeling started in my heart and spread throughout my body, keeping bad company with me as I waited for our next move.

Clairemarie called me at 5:30 p.m..

"It was the sound in his voice, Heidi...it's just tearing me apart..." She broke down sobbing.

She relayed her conversation with Michael, trying to keep her emotions in check long enough to get the words out. Michael liked the caregiver provided by the state, but Michael was not getting the full help he needed *when* he needed it. He felt like he had lost his focus without us, felt himself dying.

"Heidi, we have to go back right away."

Beth drove us to the airport and paid the six hundred dollars for our one way tickets. She agreed to drive to Portland with the harp, a modification of our initial plan. If we had left on Thursday, I would have driven my Toyota truck with the harp, Beth would have driven her Sentra, and Clairemarie would have kept us company. We would have spent Thursday night in Mt. Shasta City, arriving in Portland on Friday the 24th. Beth would have driven my truck back to California and I would have had the Sentra again for Michael's comfort. Now Beth would drive the truck solo, spend the weekend, and drive home. We would make due in Portland with Michael's friends, St. Vincent, and the state providing transportation. As I juggled all of the arrangements, I saw how much this was a part of my work as a support person. Cancer was not just a rollercoaster. I had to navigate it.

Before we left for the airport, Clairemarie showed Beth how to load the harp into the truck, reassuring her that Jiya would help. Beth was pale, her stress obvious. No matter what we said, all she could see was this exquisite, expensive instrument strung across I-5.

"Don't worry," Clairemarie tried to humor her, "it's insured. I'll risk it."

My last ditch effort to calm Beth did not work either. I reminded her of my truck's heroic history, sounding every bit like one of those commercials: 100,000 miles, a harp, and a pig later...yes, a pig. The Oakland-Berkeley Hills fire of 1991, the worst urban-wildlands fire in U.S. history, had struck dangerously close to the pet hospital where Beth and I worked. Early in the firestorm a family had evacuated their pets to the hospital as their house burned. They had a pig, a Rottweiler, and a parrot. The pig suffered from smoke inhalation. We had to evacuate the hospital two hours after she arrived and I volunteered to take her to another pet hospital. She weighed about three hundred pounds. She was just calming down from the smoke inhalation and then three people herded her to a truck, hoisted her in, and locked the door. She got upset all over again, all over my truck.

I told Beth the point of my story. With my truck, I evacuated a protesting pig in a firestorm. Driving a harp to Portland could not be harder than that.

"You'll be a hero! You'll help answer Michael's cry, '*Who will play for me?*'"

With my final statement, Beth panicked. Now the pressure was really on.

"What if the harp falls out of the truck? What if I let Michael down?" She was simply, terribly worried and would remain so until she got to Portland with the harp in one piece.

Clairemarie and I settled onto the plane at 9 p.m.. As the jet angled toward the sky, my whole being felt pulled off the ground. I sped toward Michael, suspended in air, feeling on the verge of our lives together.

We both sat meditatively until the flight attendants started pushing the beverage cart through the aisle. Hunger broke the spell of my feeling of great moment. I had not eaten in several stressful hours and now I eagerly pulled my tray down, expecting a meal. I looked forward to eating airline food. I knew I was desperate.

"What are the dinner choices?" I asked, enthused.

"We stop serving meals after 8 p.m.," the flight attendant said flatly as she handed me a half ounce bag of peanuts.

I ripped the bag open, dumped the contents into my hand, and looked at Clairemarie.

"Three hundred bucks and all I get is a stinkin' handful of peanuts!"

Clairemarie slapped my arm and we laughed at my indignation for the better part of what should have been dinner. Our laughter was our food, fortifying us once again to go on.

A steady rain welcomed us to Portland. It was midnight when we got to Michael's house. Upstairs, Clairemarie and I quietly opened the door to his room. Frigid air engulfed us as the new air conditioner droned in the background. The room, pitch black, concealed everything except Michael's head in a halo of pale green light emitted by the on-switch of the oxygen convertor next to his bed. And then I heard it for the first time. That unmistakable, indelible rhythm of the convertor, sighing in three note repetition. *Da...da...daah.*

"Michael," Clairemarie said, "I'm here now."

He answered weakly.

"Heidi's here, too."

"Good."

I stepped up to him and kissed him, remaining still in the dark for several minutes. By virtue of my presence, I helped him.

"I feel like you two should have some time alone now. I'll see you in the morning, Michael. I love you."

"Love you, too," he whispered.

I stroked his head then left the room.

Clairemarie joined me within an hour. We went to the kitchen to talk, and finally, eat.

"Oh, yuck!" I stood with the refrigerator door open. "Oh, God, Clairemarie, this is *disgusting*." I pulled out an open container of tofu with a rotten, unpeeled black banana floating in the filmy water.

"What else is in here?" She wondered out loud.

"Look at this," Clairemarie said with dismay. "Look at all this rancid oil and white sugar and fruit mixed with god-knows-what. He can't digest any of this."

"That looks like petrified oatmeal." I said as Clairemarie held onto a spoon solidified in the bowl.

"What happened to all of the things you showed the caregiver to make for Michael? What happened to all the things you cooked before we left?"

"I don't know," she shook her head.

"No wonder he called us back early. And this is only the refrigerator." I stomped around the kitchen. "Clairemarie, we've only been gone four full days. Only four days! We have to turn Michael's strength around again and this time he's in much worse shape."

"It's a good thing we came back tonight."

"We've only been gone *four days*," I couldn't stop repeating myself. "He's on oxygen all the time now. He was hardly using it when we left last Friday."

"Well, he was going for it more, though."

"Yeah, but..."

"Go get some sleep," Clairemarie handed me some fresh bread and cheese excavated from the fridge.

"Yeah, you're right. What are you going to do?"

"I'm going to stay with Michael."

We made our way back upstairs. I fell asleep to the whisperings of oxygen *da...da...daaah...*

Clairemarie slipped out of his room in the morning.

"Is he up yet?" I asked.

"Yeah, just go in. He's doing better, but he doesn't want to be alone. I'll be quick in the shower."

"Take your time."

"No. I'll be back in five or ten minutes."

I buttoned my sweater and went in to say good morning. Michael sat on the edge of the bed, expecting me.

"Hey, you," I said warmly.

"I'm so glad you're here!" He cried as I held him.

"I promised you. I'm so glad we came back last night. We got here as fast as possible."

Michael kept crying.

"Beth will be here tomorrow."

"Oh, that's really good."

"And she's bringing Clairemarie's harp for you, too."

"Wonderful," Michael sighed, adjusting the oxygen tubing on his face.

"Do you want me to adjust your leg brace?"

"Uh huh."

I unfastened the velcro straps from top to bottom. As the brace released, I noticed that Michael's foot and ankle were swollen.

"Michael, did you know that your foot is swollen?"

"No," he said, concerned.

"Can you feel your foot?"

"Yes, it feels o'kay."

"Good. I'm going to massage it for awhile. We should do this throughout the day to help the swelling go down. I'm going to put your brace back on less tightly and give you some Lasix since that worked in the hospital when your legs swelled."

139

"Right. I don't want this to get worse. Rub my leg before you put the brace on again, though."

I massaged his thigh as hard as I could since Michael felt relief with the pressure. Massaging him was hard labor for me. I doubted that I would make it through his illness and still have opposable thumbs. My hands were barely strong enough to apply so much pressure for as long as he wanted--for most of the hours in the day.

"Twelve years ago, when it was this bad, I kept asking myself, *what's the point, what's the point...*"

The tiredness in his voice disturbed me.

"And you made it through twelve years ago and you can make it through now," I said, serious but enthusiastic.

"Yeah."

"You've got a lot of help."

Michael nodded.

Clairemarie came back in the room, toweling her hair. She asked me to get Michael's next dose of percoset. When I picked up the bottle, I counted the tablets. Michael did not have enough left to make it through the weekend. With all of our comings and goings, a timely refill had slipped through the cracks. I called Dr. Mastanduno's office, left a message that Michael needed a percoset refill to get through the weekend. Simple. We waited for Dr. Mastanduno to return our call. He didn't. No problem, doctors are busy. Late in the afternoon, Clairemarie had me put in calls to all three of his offices. We kept waiting.

In the meantime, Michael was regaining his focus, bouncing back. Because he felt so good, I almost felt that I had come back prematurely. But returning when we did was the very reason for his health.

"Michael," Clairemarie said, "We aren't doing enough to stop the cancer. Besides the chemo, we need to be more aggressive cleansing your body."

"Yes," he said, listening intently, taking swigs from a bottle of Malox.

She meant diet, which had lapsed in our absence, a variety of herbs which she discussed with his doctors who did not know if herbs would help but also didn't did not think they would hurt, and she meant, of course, enemas.

Clairemarie would not leave Michael now except to run to the bathroom or kitchen. We got a lot of help with chores from Michael's close friend, Bill, who had taken over Michael's fencing classes in the Spring of 1991. Bill had just had the misfortune of losing his job, but the timing was auspicious in terms of his friendship with Michael. Bill took an active role in Michael's care, willing to help with whatever needed to be done. Since I was without my car now, he always helped with errands. He was as content to sit with Michael as he was to sit alone in the living room. Anything. Anytime.

Bill, a father of three energetic children, had his hands full with his own family. He frequently took his children with him on errands. He never put any pressure on Michael. We never once heard or felt any hint of annoyance or complaint as we sent him far across town for special supplies or piled him with four-foot stacks of laundry drenched in the pungent smell of chemotherapy-sweat.

Bill responded to Clairemarie's concern that we were burdening him by saying, "I'm willing to do anything if it helps relieve Michael's pain in the slightest way." And he was always happy to do so.

We still could not reach Dr. Mastanduno on Friday and Dr. Frank was out of town at a conference. Clairemarie, Michael, and I decided that I would go to the St. Vincent pharmacy on Saturday and try to get the refill based on Michael's ongoing status as a patient.

Beth arrived late in the afternoon, exhausted, with the harp in one piece. A passing jogger helped Clairemarie move the harp up the uneven, stepped walkway, up the porch stairs, and into the living room. The stairs to Michael's room remained to be conquered.

Beth walked in Michael's room and he smiled broadly. He stood in his usual position, arms folded, resting against his stereo cabinet, head on his arms.

"Would you like to give me a back rub?"

She worked on his shoulder muscles.

"I brought you a present, Michael."

"Neat."

"Here, take a look." Beth gave him a shower curtain with colorful Rainforest frogs on it.

"I love it."

Clairemarie hung the curtain up. Michael, in the days to come, spent many hours in the bathroom, admiring the frogs while Clairemarie gave him enemas, washed him, or stood with him by the sink, running cold water over his hands which for unknown reasons brought Michael relief.

Beth and I drove to St. Vincent on Saturday morning.

"I could drive this route with my eyes closed," I said.

"Please, don't."

I had everything memorized, where to avoid the ruts and pot holes so that Michael had a smooth, comfortable ride. He always remained calm from Southeast Portland, over the Burnside Bridge, past Powell's Books, onto Southwest Barnes Road. My own stress was in the service of his relaxation.

Beth waited in the lobby while I went into the pharmacy, chasing the elusive percosets. I handed the pharmacist Michael's Medicaid card and made my request in dismay as the pharmacist shook his head. He could not fill the prescription without the doctor's signature.

"I have to have these pills. My brother has metastatic bone cancer! He won't make it through the weekend without these!"

The pharmacist checked his computer, checked the pharmacy, called his coworkers who were off duty to see if they knew anything about filling this prescription. Nothing. Next, he paged Dr. Mastanduno, but Dr. Mastanduno could not give this narcotic prescription over the phone. I was ready to go to the fourth floor and find an oncology nurse to help me, when the pharmacist told me to go to the Family Medical Care Unit where Michael was seen by Dr. Frank.

The FMCU sent me to the emergency admitting nurse who saw my despair and anger at the bureaucracy and reassured me that she would take care of everything. She tracked down Michael's file, found a resident on duty, and wrote out a prescription for twenty percosets, enough to last until his appointment with his doctor on Tuesday. I trotted back to the pharmacy and was on my way in five minutes, feeling that a day with Michael was not all lost.

Beth and I returned to Michael's house, less than four hours after our quest began.

"These took a lot of effort," I said to him, " but it's taken care of."

"So I understand."

I was faced now, still, with the same considerations that had led me to go back to the Bay Area the week before. Still nothing yet from the federal government, still nothing from the state for caregiver expenses. Michael had the best caregiver, Clairemarie, and he had his friends like Bill to help with backup work. He himself was in much better shape than the night of our emergency flight and although he was as realistic as ever, saying he could be dead in two weeks, he was just as positive, saying he was still going to beat this. Seeing how focused he was, especially with Clairemarie, helped me decide to go home with Beth and work for another week or so.

"I'm really going to miss you, Michael," I said, doubting my decision.

"I'm really going to miss you, too."

"I'll be back right away if anything happens."

"I know."

Clairemarie, Beth, Michael, and I sat in his dark, air conditioned room, Saturday night, talking for hours, relaxed, happy.

Michael had a dream that night. He was given a pill and told that if he took it he would be completely healed. He had the dream three times and awoke refreshed, excited.

Beth and I drove home on that lucky note, Sunday morning, but I spent the whole trip having second thoughts, worried that I had just made a terrible mistake.

Chapter 17 Totentanz

June 6, 1992

I cannot count the scenes that I have played out on the stage that is my mind. This one is choreographed for bliss, that one for bravado, and that one for anguish. Here is one full of melodrama. Oh wait, how about some grand humor? Oh yes, some sparse sets and cast: just a bed and those closest to me. Well, why not the grand largess with all my grateful friends and family, glad as I make final gifts of this or that possession, sharing one last time before I give one last gift--the gift of my mortal being to the freeing ministrations of death. For a score, I chose the *Dies ire* from Mozart's *Requiem*. Or another time, it is Orpheus' lament from Monteverdi's *Orfeo*. J.S. Bach's final work, the elegant chorale prelude *In Greatest Need, I Call Upon Thee* subtitled *Herewith Do I Come Before Thine Throne* also makes a wonderful piece of background music as I try to envision my final moments before I die.

Something as simple as an unfavorable pelvic CAT scan can unleash the most macabre ballet of death images in even the most serene of spirits (which I do not have), shaking even the most indomitable of wills (not that mine is). I may be full of fight and can keep my sense of humor under the worst of circumstances, but Wednesday's report did more than disappoint me. It made me hear that little voice that always asks the same and final question: "Michael, how do you want to die?"

I have chosen. I shall dance at my death. I shall dance with death. And together we shall dance on the smiles of those I love to the music of their laughter. Our hearts and souls shall be the stage of my last dance, replete with a troupe of memories swirling by. It shall be a wonderful ballet, this dance of death, and when the curtain falls on this great tapestry of love, then, dear God, let any tear that may be shed be a tear of joy.

I hope I dance well. I hope we all dance well.

.

Chapter 18 The Last Word

My phone rang at 3 a.m., Wednesday morning.

"Heidi, are you awake?" Clairemarie's voice, soft, concerned.

"What's wrong?" I sat up in bed.

"Listen, I think you'd better come back right away. I called 911 and the paramedics were here. They just left."

"Oh, God, what happened?"

"I gave Michael one dose of this new drug for his lungs and he went so far out it's like we lost him. I didn't know what else to do except call 911."

"How is he now?"

"I can't reach him, Heidi. He looks like he's almost in a coma. The paramedic took me out of the room and said, 'Do you understand what's happening?' I said, 'I think so...' He said this is what people look like when they're really close to death. I'm calling you now in case Michael goes really fast."

"O'kay," I stumbled, "I'll get a flight as soon as I can." I had planned to drive in a day or two after she had called Tuesday night with the CAT scan results--more metastasis in his lungs.

"What medication did you give him?"

"Ativan." A tranquilizing drug to help relax his breathing.

"It sounds like his body can't metabolize it," I said. "Oh, God, Clairemarie this is a nightmare and I'm wide awake."

"Heidi, your sister, Cheryl called last night, too. So many people called yesterday...Cheryl's speech was really broken. She knows the results of yesterday's tests and she'll be here on Friday."

After the doctor's appointment on Tuesday, Michael had gone home in silence and did not speak for three hours.

Clairemarie had told me plaintively, Tuesday evening, "You know how Michael likes to exercise and do as much as he can on his own. It took him almost two hours to get from the car to his bedroom upstairs. His spirit is so strong, but his body..." She trailed off, not needing to say it.

"He finally spoke when we were in the bathroom. He said, 'You do realize what Mastanduno meant?' 'Yes, I know.' 'Well, I'll just have to heal myself.'"

Michael did not feel that he could survive a trip to Germany. Travel to an alternative therapy center, the likes of which Clairemarie was still researching, posed the same risk.

Now I sat in the cool dead of night, ready to take flight. Clairemarie continued about Cheryl.

149

"She's afraid she'll never see him again if she doesn't come now. Her husband and the boys are staying home. She just wants to be here and help out."

"I'm really glad she's coming. I'll call her this morning and give her an update. And I'll call you back and tell you when I'll be arriving."

We said goodbye and I started calling airlines. I booked a flight to Portland, arriving mid-morning. My big gray cat, Sonny, sat on the Yellow Pages, licking the tears off my face until I calmed down enough to pack.

Cheryl would fly, too, if Michael did not come around. She had stayed in touch with him with regular phone calls. Cheryl, the middle child, married to her high school sweetheart, with two little boys, Jeffrey, four, and Mark, three, and a career in the Navy as an Optometrist based in San Diego. Ready to fly.

My trip to Portland passed, an emotional blur. I walked into Michael's room. Clairemarie sat with him on the edge of the bed, holding him up.

"He can't hear you," she said, turning to me, "but this is better than when I called."

Michael's head lolled around, his eyes shut, moving under the lids.

"This might sound crazy," she went on, "but I still feel that this can change, he doesn't have to die."

"Did Dr. Mastanduno give a prognosis?"

"He said that there's nothing more he can do."

"But you still feel like there's something we can do? That Michael can do?"

"It could go either way, but I know what Michael is capable of. This can still change."

Wednesday evening, Michael regained consciousness. Clairemarie told him that she had talked to Dr. Mastanduno that day.

"I'm dying."

"That's what he says," Clairemarie spoke as gently as she could. "He says you have about a week left."

Michael silently nodded while Clairemarie encouraged him with stories of remissions that came at the eleventh hour.

She woke me up at 2:30 a.m., Thursday, with a rare request. She needed to sleep and wanted me to stay with Michael, massaging his back.

"I'll just sleep for an hour or so," she said apologetically.

"Clairemarie, please, I don't mind."

She passed out on the floor until dawn. She had arranged a row of chairs with pillows on them next to the edge of the bed, so that Michael could sit on the bed, lean over and prop his head, or stand with his head propped, but still be close to the bed. I sat down behind him, started to rub his back, feeling how thin he was. He was in the process of losing twenty-five pounds in a week.

"How much did I win?" He murmured.

"What?"

"How much did I win? I had a dream I won the lottery."

"You won the jackpot. You won the whole thing."

He did not speak anymore that night.

Michael's feet and legs were grossly swollen now. A prescription of Lasix did nothing to stop the edema from worsening. His slippers did not fit.

Clairemarie took over for me after dawn. I wandered over to the harp, resting my eyes on the ebony and gold column, then looked across the room to Michael and Clairemarie. Years seemed to have gone by since we all came together. Time had lost all ordinary sense, each day stretched, as Michael said, into "...an eternity unto itself." Thursday began another day, our endangered time together an eternity unto itself.

A nurse arrived in the late morning, the first visit from St. Vincent Homecare, a program set up for Michael by Dr. Mastanduno. Each day, from now on, a nurse would monitor Michael's vital signs, answer questions, make recommendations and equip us with what we needed. Clairemarie was offered further daily help, with household chores only, so that she could have a break, but she did not want it, rightly feeling that Michael needed someone he felt close to. And, of course, she did not want to miss "even one precious moment" with him. Each nurse, each day admired our care. All that we had to say in return was how much we loved Michael. These nurses proved themselves invaluable, offering not only medical skills but respect, good counsel, and concern. They defined their profession.

Michael's close friends from Washington, Charlotte and Henry, came to see him in the afternoon. Michael could only tolerate a maximum of three people in his room now, his physical and emotional sensitivity to his environment precluded a greater number. I sat in the living room while he had guests and began, with Charlotte and Henry's visit, to bear witness to the increasing intensity of the grief of Michael's loved ones.

Charlotte came over to me before they left.

"I know that he's your brother. I want you to know that he's our cousin."

I wanted to say something noble in return, but I simply thanked her, blinking back tears.

Most but not all of us did our best to keep a code of conduct. We broke down but not in front of Michael. It seemed unfair to burden him beyond the level of pain he already must have felt, that I can only guess at, when faced with these days of grief and goodbyes. From the living room, I saw an almost ritualized procession of grief as people came down the stairs, weeping, in open pain over Michael's rapid deterioration.

To prepare for the worst, I picked up a prescription for morphine in the late afternoon.

Exhausted, I went to bed at 10 p.m.. A knock on my door got me up within five minutes. Miwa, another of Michael's very helpful friends, stood pointing at his room next door.

"He thinks it's time."

"Time...oh..." I went into his room.

Michael sat on the edge of his bed, orchestrating everything.

"Bring me my Blue and Gold." Michael and his friend, Susan, a talented costume maker had designed this brilliant satin and lace Cavalier fencing suit based on a similar piece worn by King Charles I.

Monteverdi's *Le Orpheus* played as Michael named each piece of clothing. I scurried back and forth to his closet, bringing him the outfit piece by piece, from the white tights to the cape, from his wig with its long black curls to the black shoes with gold bows that barely fit his swollen feet. Clairemarie helped dress him and Michael stood, transformed from a late 20th century man in pajamas, ailing from cancer, into a 17th century Cavalier. He looked like Cyrano incarnate.

"Heidi, bring me my rapier," he said, popping another two percoset tablets in his mouth which made a total of, at least, six pills in the last half hour instead of two pills every four hours.

The image was complete. *Le Orpheus* rose in passionate height and Michael assumed a classic pose of the weary knight bent over his sword. I sat on the floor, at the feet of my magnificent, resplendent king, moved beyond description until I noticed Clairemarie standing at Michael's side, shoving her fist into her mouth, using every bit of self control not to laugh. Because as funny as Michael could be, there were times when you just did not laugh at him. Right now was one of those times. He took his staged death scene seriously. He felt like he was going to die tonight. *Here is one full of melodrama...*

Michael looked up, scanned each of our faces, starting with Clairemarie who stood graciously still.

154

"I thank you all for the joy you have brought into my life and I hope that I have returned the same," he said solemnly.

"You have," I said, moved to tears again, "you have so many times over."

He gave a satisfied smile, lips pressed together, and hung his head over his sword again.

Clairemarie, standing at Michael's side, passed me a note--*If he goes anywhere tonight it will be a miracle.* I could not look at her anymore and I was having a hard time looking at Michael. She breathed deeply several times, her body rocked by spasms of suppressed laughter. This went on for twenty minutes.

Michael looked up, a clammy sweat on his brow. Clairemarie took the wig off and helped him back into his pajamas. He lay down and fell into a deep, percoset induced sleep. Miwa left the room to eat watermelon in the kitchen.

Clairemarie said, "He's not going anywhere tonight."

"Except to sleep?"

"Yeah, except to sleep. I know that he doesn't think its funny, but I know that he isn't going to die tonight."

Michael woke up close to midnight.

"I need a bucket."

"You need what?" I said.

"*A bucket.*"

I grabbed a bucket and rushed to place it in front of him. He was utterly nauseous from the percosets. Clairemarie put cool washcloths on his neck and wrists and the nausea subsided. I went downstairs to eat watermelon, too.

"Why did people leave the room?" He asked her, hanging his head over the bucket.

"Because you fell into a deep sleep and they knew that you weren't dying, Michael," she kissed him. "I don't think you're going anywhere tonight."

"But I really felt it. I really felt like I was going to go."

"Well, maybe you just needed a dry run."

A dry run for death. My panache.

Friday, Michael asked for morphine instead of percoset. He fell asleep, his respiration slowing down. I sat through the morning quiet, reading in the living room, the events of last night tucked away in memory.

Clairemarie came down the stairs.

"I think he's going to go," she beckoned me.

We knelt by the side of his bed, watching him and his every peaceful breath. Pachelbel's *Canon in D* played softly, a baroque heartbeat, lyrical, passionate, singing for three people bonded by the immortality of friendship.

Michael let out a long sigh and Clairemarie and I leaned closer to him. *Oh, God, is this it?* I thought. *Has everything come to this final curtain, this great tapestry of love?* Michael's head fell to the side, facing us and then his lips curled up, a big smirk gracing his face as if to say, *Touche, I'm not going anywhere today.* He opened his eyes, blinked mischieviously at us, and

156

yawned. Clairemarie and I bowed our heads on the bed, stunned with relief.

Michael and Clairemarie rested later in the afternoon and I, again with time to read, sat in my room absorbed in a spy thriller, Lady Bear at my side.

"Heidi," Clairemarie stepped into the hall and collapsed on the floor, kicking her feet in a seizure of laughter.

"Now what? I'm just getting to the sex part in this story."

"Heidi," she tried again, but could not stop laughing.

I had lost track of how many times she came out of that room, gasping for air, trying to tell me something funny, so now I put the book down and waited for the paroxysm to subside. She told me in fits and starts that a stillness, charged with spiritual force, had permeated the room and transformed everything into a state of perfection.

"There was no cancer and no pain and no death. There was just this incredible perfection."

In the room's rarefied atmosphere, Clairemarie watched Michael drift in sleep. Suddenly, his eyes shot open and he stared at the ceiling as if a chariot had just crashed through the roof and come to get him.

"Oh, Holy God!" Michael yelled. "Oh, Holy God!"

Transfixed, Clairemarie awaited the epiphany.

"I've..." he stammered. "I've...*I've piddled!*"

"It's all right," she went to his side.

"It's disgusting. I'm disgusting," he emphasized his words with great melodrama.

"It's all right, Michael. It's just urine. It's just urine. You aren't disgusting. I love you," she stroked his head, kissing him. "I love you. This doesn't matter."

She cleaned him up, settled him in bed again, and then went out into the hall to collapse.

Cheryl flew into Portland in the early evening. Before she had left San Diego, her sons followed her into the garage, lending their support and trying to carry her suitcase.

"Michael has cancer," Jeffrey said to her. "And he just can't fight it anymore, Mom. He just can't fight it anymore, can he?"

Broken beyond words, Cheryl held her boys.

I took Cheryl now to Michael's side and he offered her his hand, the gesture he made to all of his loved ones. The two of them sat together, holding hands, Michael too weak to talk. I reflected on all of us being together for the first time in years. And probably the last, ever. What a hell of a reunion.

Cheryl saw, beyond what she had thought, just how financially strapped we were as we faced the upcoming August rent and the "etc." list of expenses--utilities, food, transportation, therapeutic supplies, etc., etc.. She started paying for whatever she could and wrote a check to Beth to help pay her credit card bill. She also made the best chicken soup, a remedy recommended by a St. Vincent homecare nurse for Michael's ever upset stomach. As a mother with young children she insisted on using her ability to get up at all hours of the night to help Clairemarie take care of Michael.

When Clairemarie felt strongly that Susan, who did not have a car and lived across town, should come over to be with Michael, Cheryl offered to pay for a cab. Before Susan arrived, Holly came over to massage Michael. Clairemarie slipped out of the room to take a shower. From my room, I heard the shower turn off and the bathroom door open after the usual five minutes. Clairemarie came pounding down the hall, a towel over her wet hair. She stormed into Michael's room, her face set with fierce determination.

"Michael," she said intensely.

He did not lift his head.

"Michael," she said again, the force in her voice rousing him. "There is an opening right now, I can feel it. This doesn't have to happen, it can still change. There is an opening, Michael, *please take it.*"

He sat straight up, alert, agreeing.

I came into the room. Holly had stopped the massage and was enthused, waving her arms.

"Yes!" Holly urged. "This cancer is bullshit! This is fucking bullshit!"

"There is an opening," Clairemarie went on. "Just because Dr. Mastanduno said you only have a week left doesn't absolutely mean that you are going to die. People have healed when they were even closer to death than what Dr. Mastanduno said you are. And *right now*, I *feel* like there is an *opening* for you."

159

"I want to take it! Yes, you're right!" Michael vigorously nodded at Clairemarie, not taking his eyes off of her, not even to blink. He had his deep enthusiasm at full throttle again.

"Ever since the doctor gave you a terminal diagnosis," Clairemarie said, "you've only eaten wafers and water. Michael, you have to stop this Christian monk diet and eat the foods that will nourish you."

"O'kay. I will. I want to take the opening."

"We want you to stay," I joined in. "We *love* you, we'll have so much more fun together!" I danced in front of him. "One big happy family!"

Cheryl came in, having been downstairs working in the kitchen. Michael's vigor amazed her. All of us were jumping or shouting for joy, Michael brightest of all, with cheers like, *Fuck cancer! There's an opening! To Michael's life! Long live the greatest brother in the world!*

Susan came to the house, brought by a friend. Our Festival of the Opening had empowered us all and Cheryl, Holly, and I, upbeat, cleared out of the room now for Michael and Susan to be together.

Paul, another close friend of Michael's, also called from New York, asking if we had received a package of a rare form of Italian chamomile tea. Michael loved this particular chamomile because it completely soothed his stomach. Paul had promised Michael that even if he had to search every Italian neighborhood in New York City, he would find this special tea, one of the few things that Michael had ever asked for. We were happy to tell Paul that a shoe box full of chamomile had arrived the day before.

Hearing Paul's soothing voice reminded me of the quiet and comfort he had given Michael during innumerable visits at the hospital and at home. Paul had only returned to New York within the last few days, having spent the last four years in college in Portland. He had been one of Michael's kendo students. Paul had plans to go to graduate school at NYU and Michael had insisted that he go.

I could see that Michael was a friend and guide to Paul the way that Clairemarie was a friend and guide to me. I understood what agony it was for Paul to leave Michael and also what respect Paul had for Michael's wishes. Watching Paul go, I had felt so grateful that I had been able to drop everything to be with Michael.

By Saturday morning, Clairemarie felt the opening close. It seemed to her that Michael was pulled away, his being attracted to some magnetic force.

"He's going to go," she thought.

Clairemarie and Cheryl stood on either side of Michael when I came into his room that morning.

"Did you swallow it, Michael?" Clairemarie asked firmly. He sat with his lips pursed, cheeks full of water.

"Michael," she tried to reach him. "Did you swallow it? Let me see. Michael, let me see." She approached his face but he jerked his head aside.

"Michael, did you swallow the morphine?" Please, open your mouth."

His glazed eyes looked at nothing. He slowly turned his head toward the center of the room and spit the water out of his mouth, narrowly missing Cheryl. I found the tablet on the floor.

"I don't know why I did that," he said, shocked. "I don't know why I did that."

We all comforted him. Clairemarie got another pill and Michael swallowed it.

Cheryl left for an overnight visit with friends in another town, planning to be back early Sunday evening. I did not feel good about the timing and told her so, but did not feel right to limit her either. I could not tell her what would happen or when. Choices were not simple, but burdened with risk.

Our Uncle Dan called from his home in New York, distraught that Michael was slipping away. Dan wished that he could fly in two directions at once because he was leaving on Sunday to be with his daughter, hospitalized in Israel. Our uncle called for the last of his intimate conversations with Michael to say *I love you*, to say *goodbye*. At first, Michael shook his head no to the phone call as he was doing at times to visitors who called or came in person. He was overwhelmed by all of the emotional pain and had recently confided his greatest agony to Clairemarie.

"I'm surrounded by everything I ever wanted in my life, by so many friends who love me, by you, a woman to be with, and Heidi is here and Cheryl...and I'm going to lose all of it. It's too late."

Dan was in tears now, talking to Clairemarie. Michael took the call.

"Yeah," he said weakly but warmly each time Dan spoke. "Yeah...yeah..."

A long last look in the mirror...the next day, the only day.

Saturday's visit from St. Vincent's homecare revealed Michael's further diminished lung capacity. The nurse told us that meant his lungs were almost filled with tumors. With cancerous bone. Because of the morphine, he was not in physical pain, but as the day wore on he was not responsive either. We felt that we had robbed him of his consciousness and that we had already lost him. Michael had always insisted on remaining conscious and without his voiced permission, we could not in right conscience continue the morphine, sending him into seeming narcotic oblivion.

Clairemarie sent me to the Yellow Pages with instructions to call every acupuncturist listed until I found someone really good who was experienced with pain management for a terminally ill cancer patient.

"You want me to call every single one?"

"Yeah, start with the A's. You'll see. Most people know each other and you'll quickly learn about who's who."

I did not even get to the middle of the alphabet when one acupuncturist led me to her teacher, the doctor who taught many of the practicing acupuncturists in Portland. Dr. Cheung. She said he was the

163

best which was good enough for me. He agreed to make a housecall at 5 p.m..

Clairemarie had weaned Michael off the morphine so he was lucid enough to verbally respond to questions when Dr. Cheung made his housecall. The session took an hour and left no doubt as to the good doctor's expertise. He spoke to me after the session, privately, saying that Michael would not die in agony and that soon, possibly a day or two, he would slip into a coma and pass on. Dr. Chueng was matter of fact, but with a calming manner, comforting.

Michael asked for morphine at 7 p.m.. Clairemarie gave it to him.

"I just had to hear it out of his own mouth."

Clairemarie and I focused on maintaining an atmosphere of love and safety for Michael. She played her harp for much of the night. I listened to the living reason why Clairemarie chose to be a harper. As she has said so many times, the harp is a symbol of grace in a graceless world. She played for Michael, dying of this rotten, graceless disease. The beautiful music, resonant with its heavenly symbols, bridged this world with the next.

Michael rested flat on his back, immobile. I had come up with a good way to move him when he needed to be cleaned. After seeing him nearly dropped once, I started using a sheet as a full body stretcher and he no longer feared that we might drop him or put too much pressure on his chest and hips. I looked into his eyes each time and told him every move we made, saying *you're all right, it's o'kay.* Since our last move Saturday night, Michael sounded like a broken Monty Python record--

164

right, right, right...o'kay, o'kay, o'kay--until the middle of the night when he stopped talking all together.

Sunday morning, I canceled the acupuncture session for the day and called Holly to cancel the massage. I invited her, instead, to come sit with Michael. I then phoned Michael's friends and told them to come. Cheryl arranged for a ride back. Beth was on the road, too, bringing my truck, driving against time to see Michael. Everyone else was away and could not be reached. When I finished the clarion phone calls, I looked at Michael, touched him.

"You're the best brother in the world. You always will be. I will always, always love you."

Holly got to the house first, then Susan and Miwa, followed by Bill in the afternoon.

Jenny, a St. Vincent homecare nurse, spent considerable time with us in the morning. St Vincent is made of people like Jenny, a consummate professional, a consummate human being. She communicated directly with Michael, making herself known to him and making him important to her. He spoke to her silently with his eyes. Then she sat down and talked with Clairemarie and me, explaining what was going on, advising us on how to proceed.

"This is called a death rattle," she described Michael's breathing to us. "It can last approximately up to seventy-two hours." She also told us that as the body shuts down there are two kinds of kidney failure, high output and low output. Michael had low output. Now I understood why we had not had to clean him much since the night before. She

165

verified that the morphine was blocking the pain. Her technical descriptions, delivered with compassion, never lost sight of Michael as a human being and never lost sight of us as the human beings who loved him.

Jenny is a nurse not a priest, but she conveyed with her particular expertise invaluable counsel and aid to the bereaved and to the dying. She did not read from any spiritual tradition other than her heart. Under my definition of hospice is her name.

Clairemarie felt deeply today that she could not play for Michael, she could only sing for him. She sat down on the bed after Jenny left and sang all day, sponging his mouth continuously with small amounts of water. Melody poured out of her, spiritual songs gathered from her worldwide travels, especially a *mantra* (divine chant) from India where the belief is held firm that the sound of a mantra at the time of death will help the spirit go to a higher or heavenly place.

Clairemarie sang, *Arut Perum Jyoti, Arut Perum Jyoti, Tanip Perum Karunai, Arut Perum Jyoti.* Translated as *Vast Grace Light, Vast Grace Light, Supreme Compassionate, Vast Grace Light.* This mantra comes from the well known Indian Saint, Ramalingam, famous for his poetry and miracles, but lesser known for his greatest act--dissolving his deathless body. Clairemarie had told the following story to Michael during his last hospitalization, showing him Ramalingam's picture. The story and the saint, preposterous to many a Western mind, deeply inspired Michael and he asked that the picture always be in his room.

Ramalingam's realization of a divine being, "Supreme Compassionate Vast Grace Light," transformed his mortal body into a deathless body. He believed that death was an accident, unnecessary. But he also saw that people did not understand this. He chose to dissolve his deathless body, releasing the atoms into the environmental totality of the human species in order to accelerate the time when people would understand and accept a deathless body. (And I thought Quantum Physics was complicated.) At this time, he promised to reappear. So, in the ultimate locked room puzzle, Ramalingam barricaded himself in his room and disappeared or, rather, dissolved. The Madras police launched an extensive investigation, suspecting foul play, but their findings were inconclusive and Ramalingam has not been seen since. Michael loved every word of it.

Ramalingam's picture sat on the pillow above Michael's head, a pastel pink silk scarf from another sacred Indian site, Meherabad, was draped over his chest. Clairemarie sang and sang and sang.

Bill came to the house in the mid-afternoon with a wooden flute. I ushered him into Michael's room and then joined Susan and Miwa downstairs. I was still considerate of the fact not to crowd the room. This was Bill's time.

He sat down on the opposite side of the bed from Clairemarie. He pressed his fist against his belly, called the *chi* or power center in martial arts, and pressed his fist against his heart, saying, "I will always remember you here and here. I will never forget you. I will always love you and I will never forget."

The time neared 5 p.m. and Cheryl would be here in fifteen more minutes. The sound of Bill playing his flute drifted downstairs. He played *Greensleeves*, off key, hitting the wrong notes, but with the best intention. When the song ended, I hurried up the stairs and from the doorway saw Bill weeping.

Just, I thought. Just now. Michael was dead.

Clairemarie sat next to him and held his hands to her heart, chanting, "*Keep going, keep going, keep going...*"

My eyes burned with tears seeing that Michael, whose only fear of death had been to die alone, was surrounded by the best of company, not just watched *as* he died but helped *to* die with our love, safety, blessed music, and guidance. I thought of how strong his fear was and how strong and triumphant was our desire to allay that fear. And then his last word echoed in my mind, a last offering that said to me, *I'm so glad you're here.*

Early in the morning, he had been alone for a few minutes when Clairemarie left the room to take a shower and I stopped my chores and went to him. As distant as he was on morphine, as silent as he had become, he rolled his head to the side when I entered the room. He looked at me and said my name and that was all. He said, *Heidi.*

Cheryl and other friends and family converged upon the house by 5:10 p.m.. Clairemarie folded Michael's hands on his chest. She and I put our arms around each other and walked outside, making room for others to be near Michael.

Clairemarie and I stood on the sidewalk outside the house, silent. Over an hour went by and then we watched the van from Portland Memorial disappear westward with his body, toward the Willamette River.

"Heid, what time is it?"

"It's six-thirty."

"Just in time for the sunrise."

"No. The sunset."

"No. It's the morning."

"No. It's the evening."

"It's the morning. Just look at the light."

"Clairemarie, it is the evening. You've been in a darkened room all day."

"That's not why. Everything feels like the dawn. Look at the light."

I did and it overwhelmed me.

"Have you ever seen such a beautiful golden dawn?" She asked.

She was right. Everything was imbued with golden light. Everything was luminous. We were luminous. We agreed that Portland did not look like Portland anymore.

"It's gorgeous," she sighed.

"It's the same as the golden light in Michael's eyes."

We stood holding each other, unable to cry, smiling, absorbed in a glory of light.

169

Chapter 19 Bridge of the Gods

A legend is told of a terrible sickness that threatened the Multnomah people. An old medicine man revealed that the sickness would pass if a maiden threw herself from a high cliff on the Big River to the rocks below. When the Chief's daughter saw the sickness on her lover's face, she went to the cliff and plunged to her death. Now, when the breeze blows through the water, a silvery stream separates from the upper falls. The misty stream fashions a form of the maiden, a token of the Great Spirit's acceptance of her sacrifice.

--Multnomah Falls Princess Legend

Michael died at 5 p.m. on August 2, 1992. He was thirty-four years old. I am forever grateful for all that he and I shared in our lives together. I am grateful that even though we had so little time from diagnosis to death, from April to August, we nonetheless had *enough* time to say everything we wanted to say to each other, to be complete in the gifts and deeds of our words for each other. *I'm so glad you're here. I love you. Neep.* Thank God one of us was not run over in the street by an applecart. I know people who have lost loved ones to sudden death and I am grateful for the four months, in 1992, and I am grateful for the twelve years from the first to the second round of cancer. I am grateful that we shared this book together.

The telephone is a big part of my grieving because Michael and I spent so much of our time long distance. When I hear the phone ring, I know Michael will never be on the line and I know that I can never call him. My Neep died.

I can never read him another passage to this book and there will be no more passages from him. Only the great passage of his life confronts me now. Never again will we cry on the phone and say, *that's really wonderful, that's us*...and that realization, again and again, every time the phone rings, is really tough. It hurts.

With all of the immediacy of my grief, including my very low phone bill, I am forever grateful that in my life and in Michael's lifetime, however young or brief it all is, we realized true brotherly and sisterly love. If anyone ever shares an ounce of the feelings that Michael and I shared that person is lucky and blessed indeed. We were and we were complete with each other.

As I write this, as I have lived it, I am twenty-nine to thirty years old and I know that this time is a critical degree in my life, in which everything that has come before now culminates. Every experience, every relationship. Every person and every place. Every doubt, every wonder. Every dream and every goal. Every fear, every pain. Every hope and every love. Life and Death. This year is shining a search light on every aspect of my life thus far and I am exposed, challenged, honed, made reflective in the brilliance of crisis and inexorable change, this rite of passage into the clarity of letting go.

Nothing is the same anymore, most definitely not me. Who or what I am, who or what I was, who or what I will be is all different, now, burned clean in the fire of time. I do not see anything as I am accustomed to seeing, but I am not pushing for a new frame of reference, a relative meaning to impose on life. Right now, I am just acknowledging that I have been branded by experiences and losses that have forever altered my being in this world, in this life, and I have quite a ways to go yet before any of these changes will integrate in my soul, heart, and mind.

Fire predominates. A fire started by Michael's death. While Michael first appeared in this world, in 1958, under the sign of Aquarius the Water Bearer, a gracious giver in the circumference of the lives of those who knew him, he disappeared under the opposite sign of Leo, a dignified, noble being borne away, in the season of the Fire Cat, from this life and its extinguished flame.

There are times now when I feel so robbed of our adult lives together that I shake one of his crutches at the starry night sky, railing at the universe because Michael died. I am still shocked by the recurrence of cancer, but now I am knocked further out of the orbit of my life because Michael died. Michael with cancer again! Oh, God, no. Michael dead! *Dead.* He's dead! He's dead! I shake his crutch at cancer and death, at the sky into which I can only imagine he vanished.

172

Shaking that old crutch, that traveled so many thousands of miles with Michael, acts as a magic wand to transport me across time and space, beyond cancer and death and my derailed orbit to the Columbia River Gorge and a wonderful bridge with a graceful arch and a 620 foot waterfall rushing behind it. I am transported to Multnomah Falls, the holy place in which we fulfilled Michael's dying wish to scatter his ashes at dawn.

The most stunning, incomprehensible moment in my life was on August 5 when I went to Portland Memorial to "pick up my brother". I knew this was not Michael. I saw him die. I saw his corpse and knew fundamentally, tacitly, and irrevocably in that moment that we are not our bodies. I sat for hours, along with Clairemarie, with his body lying in state before the cremation. I went with Clairemarie into the prep room, truly an image of a morgue, reeking of formaldehyde, filled with white porcelain wash tables and a bucket marked *viscera only*. There we undressed him from his beautiful blue and gold fencing suit.

I kept a firm grip on his sword while the funeral director elevated Michael's body out of the casket on a lift, moving him, dangling naked, over my head, to a table across the room. Again, I kept a firm grip on the sword as the most bizarre and wrenching image continued to pass before me, as the funeral director swung Michael's body back through the air and lowered him into the pine box that would soon go to the crematorium; and with that pine box the last signs of cancer, the bald head, the small hole in his chest from the Groshong catheter, and all other visible identifications of this body as Michael. And I stood, his sword in my hand, through each jarring sound as the lid was nailed on the coffin. But nothing could have been more final and strange as a brown plastic box in a velvet drawstring bag put before me on a counter, as I listened to the funeral home worker compassionately call it, "Michael".

"Are you going to be o'kay?" She asked.

"It's heavy."

"Would you like to sit down? Are you going to be o'kay?" She really was compassionate. I just could not take in Michael's boxed remains, let alone her reference to this container as Michael.

"It's just heavy. I didn't think it would be."

I did not really know what to think except that I was finding another angle on the impossibility of being only a body. This was no abstract philosophical inquiry to me. It was as tangible a confrontation as that plastic box in the velvet bag.

When I got back to Michael's house, Clairemarie was even more visibly stunned by the ashes than I was. She just sat with them in her lap, staring in awe that this ever could have been the man she so lovingly cared for, that only a few days ago she had been massaging, feeding, washing. The intensity of her round the clock caregiving now abruptly sat in her lap. Here was a bag of bones where there was once a man, the man she utterly loved. The tremendous emotional impact of the transition from Michael's vital life to *this* left her wide-eyed, telling everyone in the room, "My mind just can't take this in." And so she sat there, staring, for a very long time.

For Michael's close friends, in Germany and Washington state, who could not make it to the Gorge, it was a natural choice to send some of Michael's ashes to them. I heard in depth of the reception given Michael's remains in Germany. His best friend, Hans-Joachim, in Munich, described his travels and experiences in a letter that was evocative of his very deep love for the friend who "founded our family." Michael had introduced Hans-Joachim to his wife, Lonnie, and Michael became the first adult friend of their son, Martin, four years old at the time of Michael's passing. Martin was so angelically beautiful that he looked like he had stepped right out of a Botticelli painting. This family of friends wrote:

...I reflected on an appropriate place to scatter Michael's ashes. I passed through the time of my life with Michael, the honor and gratitude we owed him and found a solution. We divided the ashes into three parts. The first part we brought out to the former monk's cemetery of the former Abbey Church of Fuerstenfeld, where Michael all his lifetime had been with great pleasure. Before Michael's ashes came to its peace, we listened to an organ concert (it was the holiday of St. Mary's Ascension, August 15th) with old music of Portugal. That organ concert was played on the organ we--Michael and I--recorded in 1980, when Michael felt the

175

affection of the cancer for the first time. Michael had made the acquaintance of the organ some months earlier and was deeply impressed. To touch a historical monument, to listen to an instrument, which was erected in its oldest parts in ca. 1630 and in its main part 1736, seemed to be an incarnation of the dream he had. We examined the technology of the instrument, I tried to explain the 'inside story' to Michael, he played and listened, he listened and played.

...the church is devoted to St. Mary's Ascension. The abbey of Fuerstenfeld is the "original" burial cloister of the Wittelsbacher, the family of the Bavarian Dukes. Michael and I visited the crypt under the church and we were near the breath of the middle ages...near to Emperor Ludwig the Bavarian, or Duke Ludwig the Severe.

Very near to all of them Michael rests now. We brought out his ashes at the outer side of the choir's vertex (to the east). So he rests "under" the altar, not too close, but near enough to hear the organ, to imagine St. Mary's ascension, to reflect the life of Jesus Christ, to reflect the life of human beings, [the monks]...buried there over centuries.

...One day later...we attended another organ concert as a memorial...with toccatas by Muffat, Speth and Bach...Martin listened to both concerts the whole time. With our bicycles we went after that to the forest area between Schaeftlarn and Percha. This part of the Upper Bavarian countryside Michael loved all his lifetime and spent, in Percha

176

in August/September...last year, very happy and hopeful days. From
the point where we brought out the ashes, one may see the Alps. Martin
was with us and asked to bring out, also, a handful of ashes.

...we offered our reference to Michael as a descendant of the Jewish
religion...When I heard the first time, about 14 years ago, about his love
of a country...which brought incredible misfortune, injury and harm over
the Jews, it touched me inextinguishably in my inner being.

[We went]...by railroad and bicycles to Moenchsdeggingen...there still
exits a small Jewish cemetery...

Besides us two other friends of Michael's (Eberhard...and
Bernhard...) accompanied Michael's relics on their very last journey in this
world...

...Over all sadness, to renounce Michael for all of our future, we felt
the quiet comfort and contentment, laying over the cemetery in the
naturalness of that paradisian meadow, out of which the monuments of
human transitoriness grow up. We were quiet, when we all scattered
Michael's ashes.

I was so moved by the depth of feeling and thought that Hans-
Joachim revealed in his letter and by how far reaching yet always
inclusive is this tapestry of love. At a time when xenophobia and Neo-

Nazi violence were again on the rise in Germany, of which Jewish cemeteries were among the prime targets, I found even more power and grace in the acts of these good people who consecrated their friend.

Michael was crazy about Martin. When Michael was in Munich, in the summer of 1991, to have his knee prosthesis replaced, he spent hours showing Martin how to play the synthesizers brought over from the States. These instruments subsequently became Martin's inheritance.

One of the most poignant moments during Michael's recurrence of cancer was when he heard that Martin, on a walk with his parents, pointed to Klinikum rechts der Isar and said, "That's where Michael lives."

Martin's statement touched Michael to the core and he cried for this painful but lifesaving *home*, realizing just how much of his life he did live at that hospital, through his first round of cancer and the subsequent repairs to and replacement of his knee prosthesis. From the words of a young boy, it all came rushing back to him in the time, again, when cancer dominated his life.

Shortly after Michael's passing, Martin came to his parents and said, "Michael died. I'm going to cry now." And he burst into tears.

Before any of Michael's remains were sent to anyone, however, Clairemarie made sure that the remains would not arrive in crude form. We knew beyond a doubt that those ashes were Michael's when we saw the remains of his prosthetic, orthopedic hardware, the screws and bolts and hinges, mixed in with the remains of his bones. While I made bad jokes about finding Michael's loose screw and shouldn't we all be so lucky, Clairemarie was aghast at the thought of sending his pulverized, hardware littered remains to his friends.

We learned more about cremation than we ever wanted to know. We found out that not all cremation processes give the same final result. The methods either pulverize the boney remains into small bits or grind the boney remains into an ashen powder. We got the small bits method with hardware and Clairemarie, rightfully so, could not bear to send a bunch of chunks to Michael's friends.

After she got up from staring at the ashes, she went to the kitchen and sorted out a small portion of Michael's remains. Then she opted for the ashen powder method with the available kitchen tools.

"Michael, I'm still serving your body," I heard her say over the grinding roar of the mini-food processor.

"Don't breathe that!" I yelled as a cloud of white dust gushed past her face. "It's probably full of chemo. Get a surgical mask." But whether the dust had any remnant of chemo or not, she just diligently kept on working.

Once the job was done, we had two lovely jars wrapped in Florentine paper ready to go far away to people and places that were special to Michael. Clairemarie also saved a small amount of Michael's ashes to take with her the next time she goes to India. Michael wanted to go there so much and someday some part of him will.

As the end of July had approached and Michael's health deteriorated rapidly, Clairemarie said, "Michael, please don't die on my birthday."

"When is it?

"August sixth."

"O'kay, I won't."

He asked her several times after that, "When is your birthday? August sixth? O'kay."

True to his word, he did not die on her birthday, but as things turned out, on August 6, we went to the Gorge to scatter his ashes.

A small group of us got up at 3:30 a.m. and drove out to Multnomah Falls. We hiked up to the bridge in the dark, which a lot of Portlanders lovingly call, Bridge of the Gods (even though, technically, Bridge of the Gods is located further down the scenic highway) and there, in the cool of the morning, we waited in silence.

At the moment of dawn with the light casting its early illuminating glow on the cliffs, water, and bridge we began to sing *Old and Wise* and, handful by handful, we scattered Michael's ashes over the bridge to the rippling pool below. All the elements of our material existence merged at this point of departure: the fire of the dawn; the water of the falls; the air of our voices, singing; and the earth of Michael's drifting dust.

The song, *Old and Wise*, sounded overwhelmingly like a direct statement from Michael. Bill, his wooden flute and *Greensleeves* set aside, had felt compelled to sing *Old and Wise* on the night that Michael died. It was heartbreaking to hear the song and Bill's strong, passionate tenor because the words and music were such a vivid portrayal of Michael. That night of August 2, we sang it over and over again.

By the time I got to the bridge on the 6th, I knew the song by heart like I knew Michael by heart. As we sang and scattered his ashes, while the morning light turned the water to gold, I understood from this most poetic and releasing moment, for all that has been burned away from me, that the Bridge of the Gods is the bridge to my memory that I will never burn. As the waters wash away the bodily remains of my brother, my memory and love span time and space, connecting me with him still like a bridge to the gods.

Appendix

Questions?

I inevitably wondered how Michael got cancer, but the barrage of questions that came from various people and that arose, at times, out of my own mind, were questionable themselves. Before Michael's recurrence, I occasionally subscribed to one of the popular, distorted notions that "you create your own reality".

When I got on these jags and tried to come up with a unified field theory of Michael's life in light of his illness, I would think that his self-destructive attitudes, like his low self-esteem, contributed to his cancer in 1980. The fact that I have never met anyone with or without cancer who does not have at least one self-destructive attitude at some time in his or her life did not stand in my way. I just overlooked the flaw in my own reasoning that self-destructive attitudes do not necessarily make you self-destruct and get cancer.

I do not wish to take issue here with the complexity of mind-body interactions, but rather to examine one of the dangers in oversimplifying such a dynamic. Oversimplification makes certainties where none really exist, makes easy answers out of a complexity of valid as well as controversial influences.

Michael and I encountered a certain list of questions, most asked quite causally like being asked the time of day, as if the questions were an implicit agreement. *What caused Michael's cancer? How did he give it to himself? What did he do wrong in his life? What was he doing with his lifestyle? His diet? His body image? His emotions? His anger? His intimate relationships? All of the above? Some of the above?* These questions are endless variations on the same theme, that Michael *did* something to bring cancer on himself.

Michael did follow a lifestyle that was rich in physical exercise, meditation, and friendships. He also had tremendous physical, mental, and spiritual vitality. People had a hard time keeping up with him even when he was sick because he was so highly energetic. Perhaps, always perhaps, Michael could have done certain things to strengthen his immune system, to lower his risk of disease, by eating less from his four food groups (meat, cheese, beer, and chocolate), having a healthier body image, being in a stable, loving relationship, being less lonely, more this, less of that. But in no way can it be said that he would have prevented or lessened the impact of his progenitor bone cells growing like wildfire, awry. And while many causes of cancer are known even these factors do not fully explain why some people succumb at a particular time in life to a particular type of cancer and others succumb at a different time or not at all. Michael did a lot for himself regardless of whatever liabilities--like

184

everyone else--he may have had, but he succumbed to one of the myriad and very aggressive forms of cancer.

The questions that I have listed are, at their root, only one question: *why was he at fault?* Looking at my own past tendencies to ask such things, I have realized how impossible it is to draw conclusions from this type of inquiry. Instead I found it vitally important when Michael's very life was again on the line, to question the questions themselves, to get at the hidden motivations which serve no beneficial purpose, but only judge and make an ill person feel like he or she gave him or herself this disease, that he or she did something wrong and is wrong.

The judgment inherent in asking this type of question is based on a motivation to rationalize not only uncertainty but to defend yourself from the real threat that cancer holds for all of us. This fear-based questioning generates guilt and a sense of failure--as if having a life-threatening illness is not hard enough to deal with already. Rationalizing keeps the illness and our own mortality at bay. It also keeps the ill person at bay and prevents fully entering into the moment of loving someone with a true depth of compassion. Indeed, a warped insistence on having a "positive attitude" becomes its own opposite: a negative judgment.

I could not bear to let anything stand in the way of loving Michael, of being there for him in the midst of his suffering, and that meant my own fears and desires to hang the reason for his illness on a peg of distorted personal responsibility. I felt barbaric pointing a finger at Michael.

When I caught on to what was really behind questioning Michael's behavior, I imagined asking the same thing of the dogs and cats that I deal with in my veterinary work because I have seen so many animals with various types of cancer, some with osteosarcoma, the same as what Michael had.

Spike, you're a German Shepherd with metastatic bone cancer. Did you feel inadequate as man's best friend? Did you feel like you couldn't be as good as Lassie? Did you eat Kal Kan instead of Science Diet? How about you, Muffin? You're a young tabby with adenocarcinoma. Did you feel abandoned by your mother? Were you tired of having nine lives to live?

Ludicrous.

Cancer is a highly complex disease. It is many diseases really with many causes and I cannot reduce it to a set of speculative rationalizations because I am afraid and am subtly trying to defend myself from getting cancer as unexpectedly as Michael did--or Spike or Muffin. I have had to come to emotional terms with this not intellectually sentimental terms. I must be emotionally ready to ask a tougher and a more interactive question based on how I live in this world. In a larger context, I must ask myself not *what did he do to get it?* but *when will I?* Because the odds keep stacking up against all of us.

Right now, in the United States, cancer is the number 2 killer disease, behind heart disease. The rate of incidence of almost all kinds of cancers is staggering, and cannot entirely be attributed to increasing longevity, better record keeping, better diagnostics, or control of other diseases.

This does not comfort me nor should it. It also does not scare me into feeling helpless. Everything does not cause cancer and much can be done to reduce one's risk. I must take a look in the mirror at myself which means taking a look at the carcinogens under my sink, in the car I drive, or the food I eat. How, I ask myself, am I contributing to the rise in cancer just by the way I live everyday as a member of this society of consumption and pollution? That *is* my responsibility. As insurmountable as the massive level of changes may be to start counteracting the damage done to our planet by radiation, depletion of the ozone, pesticides, and on and on, I know one thing: the changes start with myself. Without question.

About the Author

Michael was a modern day renaissance man, a musician and composer, writer, translator, swordsman, computer engineer, historian, and world traveler.

Heidi is a freelance writer. She lives in the San Francisco Bay Area.

Connect online:

Email: hzawelevsky @gmail.com with Tapestry of Love as the subject.

Cover photo by Heidi Zawelevsky

Made in the USA
Coppell, TX
22 April 2023